03/2008

Remember to focus
on <u>Him</u>.

Lorraine

The Ideals
Treasury
of Faith *and*
Inspiration

FAITH

Lord, give me faith to live from day to day;
With tranquil heart to do my simple part,
And, with my hand in Thine, just go Thy way.

Lord, give me faith to trust, if not to know;
With quiet mind in all things Thee to find,
And, childlike, go where Thou wouldst have me go.

Lord, give me faith to leave it all to Thee.
The future is Thy gift; I would not lift
The veil Thy Love has hung 'twixt it and me.

JOHN OXENHAM

THE IDEALS
TREASURY
of FAITH *and*
INSPIRATION

PHOTOGRAPHY BY DENNIS FRATES

And Jesus said unto them, Because of your unbelief: for verily I say unto you, If ye have faith as a grain of mustard seed, ye shall say unto this mountain, Remove hence to yonder place; and it shall remove; and nothing shall be impossible unto you.

—MATTHEW 17:20

IDEALS PUBLICATIONS
NASHVILLE, TENNESSEE

ISBN 0-8249-5863-2
Published by Ideals Publications
A division of Guideposts
535 Metroplex Drive, Suite 250
Nashville, Tennessee 37211
www.idealsbooks.com

Printed and bound in Italy

Library of Congress CIP data on file

Publisher, Patricia A. Pingry
Associate Publisher, Peggy Schaefer
Editor, Julie K. Hogan
Art Director, Eve DeGrie
Production, Patrick McRae
Copy Editors, Lisa Ragan, Melinda Rathjen
Research Assistants, Mary P. Dunn, Margaret A. Hogan

Cover photograph: Heceta Lighthouse, Devil's Elbow State
Park, Oregon
Title page: Mono Lake, California
Photograph right: Yellow wildflowers along the coast of
Bandon, Oregon

Artwork by Glenda Puhek

10 9 8 7 6 5 4 3 2 1

ACKNOWLEDGMENTS

FRERE, WALTER HOWARD, "A Prayer of Faith;" JARRETT, BEDE, "Our Endless Home;" PATON, ALAN, "A Prayer of Faith;" from *The Complete Book of Christian Prayer*. Copyright © 1995 by SPCK, used by permission of Continuum International Publishing Group. ANDERSON, BEVERLY J. "Hope" used by permission of Daisy Kerr. ANDERSON, TERRY. "Small Graces" from *Changed Lives*. Copyright 2002 by Guideposts. Used by permission. BARCLAY, WILLIAM. "A Prayer" from *More Prayers of the Plain Man*, published by Fontana Press/HarperCollins, UK. BARTON, MARIE. "Like A Candle" from *Best Loved Unity Poems*. Unity School of Christianity. BRISCOE, JILL. "The Ultra-Suede Ladies" from *Thank You for Being a Friend*. Copyright © 1980 by Jill Briscoe. Used by permission of Anne E. Burket. CROWELL, GRACE NOLL. "Hope" from *Songs of Hope*. Copyright © 1938 by Harper & Brothers, renewed 1966 by Grace Noll Crowell and "A Prayer for Courage" from *Flame in the Wind*. Copyright © 1930, 1934 by Harper & Brothers, renewed 1952 by Grace Noll Crowell. Reprinted by permission of HarperCollins Publishers Inc. FRANK, ANNE. Excerpts from *The Diary of Anne Frank: The Critical Edition* by Anne Frank. Copyright © 1986 by Anne Frank-Fonds, Basle/Switzerland for all texts of Anne Frank. Used by permission of Doubleday, a division of Random House, Inc. HALL, MYRTLE. "A New Day" from *Every Man Is a Brother Lord* by Myrtle Hall. Copyright by the Church Mission Society. Used by permission of CMS (UK). KENNEDY, PAMELA. "The Joy of Friendship" used by permission of the author. LAWRENCE, J. B. "I Believe" from *The Best Loved Religious Poems* by James G. Lawson, Fleming Revell, 1933. Used by permission of Baker Book House Company. MARSHALL, CATHERINE. "Entering In" from *Beyond Ourselves*. Copyright © 1961 by Catherine Marshall. Published by Avon Books by arrangement with McGraw-Hill. "To Comfort All That Mourn" from *To Live Again*. Copyright © 1957, renewed 1985 and 1996 by Catherine Marshall. Published by Fawcett World Library by arrangement with McGraw-Hill Book Company. MARSHALL, PETER. "A Prayer for Courage" and "A Prayer of Peace" from *The Prayers of Peter Marshall*, Copyright © 1949, renewed 1954 and 1982 by Catherine Marshall. Used by permission of Baker Book House. MERTON, THOMAS. "A Prayer of Peace" from *Thoughts in Solitude*. Copyright © 1956, 1958 by the Abbey of Our Lady of Gethsemani, renewed 1986 by the Trustees of the Thomas Merton Legacy Trust. Published by Farrar, Straus & Giroux, Inc. OLSON, ENID MARTEL. "A Prayer for Hope" from *Poems of Faith for the Christian*

Year by Enid Martell Olson. Copyright © 1959 Augsburg Publishing House. Used by permission of Augsburg Fortress. POWERS, MARGARET FISHBACK. "Footprints" from *Footprints*. Copyright © 1964 by the author. Published by HarperCollins Publishers Ltd. (Canada). RICE, HELEN STEINER. "Daily Prayers Dissolve Your Cares," copyright © 1968 by the Helen Steiner Rice™ Foundation. "Look on the Sunny Side", copyright © 1971 by the Helen Steiner Rice™ Foundation. Used by permission of The Helen Steiner Rice™ Foundation, Cincinnati, Ohio. ROSE, DARLENE DIEBLER. "Evidence Not Seen" from *Evidence Not Seen*. Copyright © 1988 by Darlene Diebler Rose. HarperCollins Publishers. SCHAEFFER, EDITH. "How We Bought L' Abri" from *L' Abri*. Copyright © 1969 by Edith Schaeffer, Tyndale House edition by arrangement with The Norfolk Press. Current revised version by Crossway Books. Copyright ©1992 by Edith Schaeffer. Used by permission of the publisher. SIMSIC, WAYNE. "Foundations of Faith" from *Faith: Daily Prayers for Virtue*. Saint Mary's Press, Winona, MN, 1997. Used by permission of the publisher. STIDGER, WILLIAM A. "Who Will Lead Me Into Edom." Used by permission of William S. Hyland. TEN BOOM, CORRIE. "The Best Is Yet to Be" from *My Father's House* by Corrie ten Boom and Carole C. Carlson. Copyright © 1976 by Corrie ten Boom and Carole C. Carlson. Published by Fleming Revell Co., Baker Book House. STRONG, PATIENCE. "Hope Dwells Ever in the Soul" from *Paths of Promise* by Patience Strong. Copyright © 1951 by Patience Strong. Used by permission of Rupert Crew, Ltd. "Sun on Stone" from *The Book of Comfort and Joy*, Copyright © 1981 by Ideals Publications. Our sincere thanks to the following authors whom we were unable to locate: ALLEN, JAMES. for "The Lamp of Faith," DOUCE, MS. for "A Prayer of Peace"; the Estate of ANNIE J. FLINT , for "What God Hath Promised" and "We see Jesus; GANNETT, WILLIAM CHANNING, for "The Stream of Faith"; KEELING, MILDRED, for "God's World"; NEUMANN, CASPER, for "A Prayer for Comfort"; ORCHARD, WILLIAM E., for "A Prayer for Hope"; the Estate of John, Oxenham for "Faith" and "Credo" and "Love's Prerogative"; ROBBINS, SAMUEL DOWSE, for "Father, Take My Hand."

All possible care has been taken to fully acknowledge the ownership and use of each selection. If any mistakes or omissions have occurred, they will be corrected in subsequent editions, provided notification is sent to the publisher.

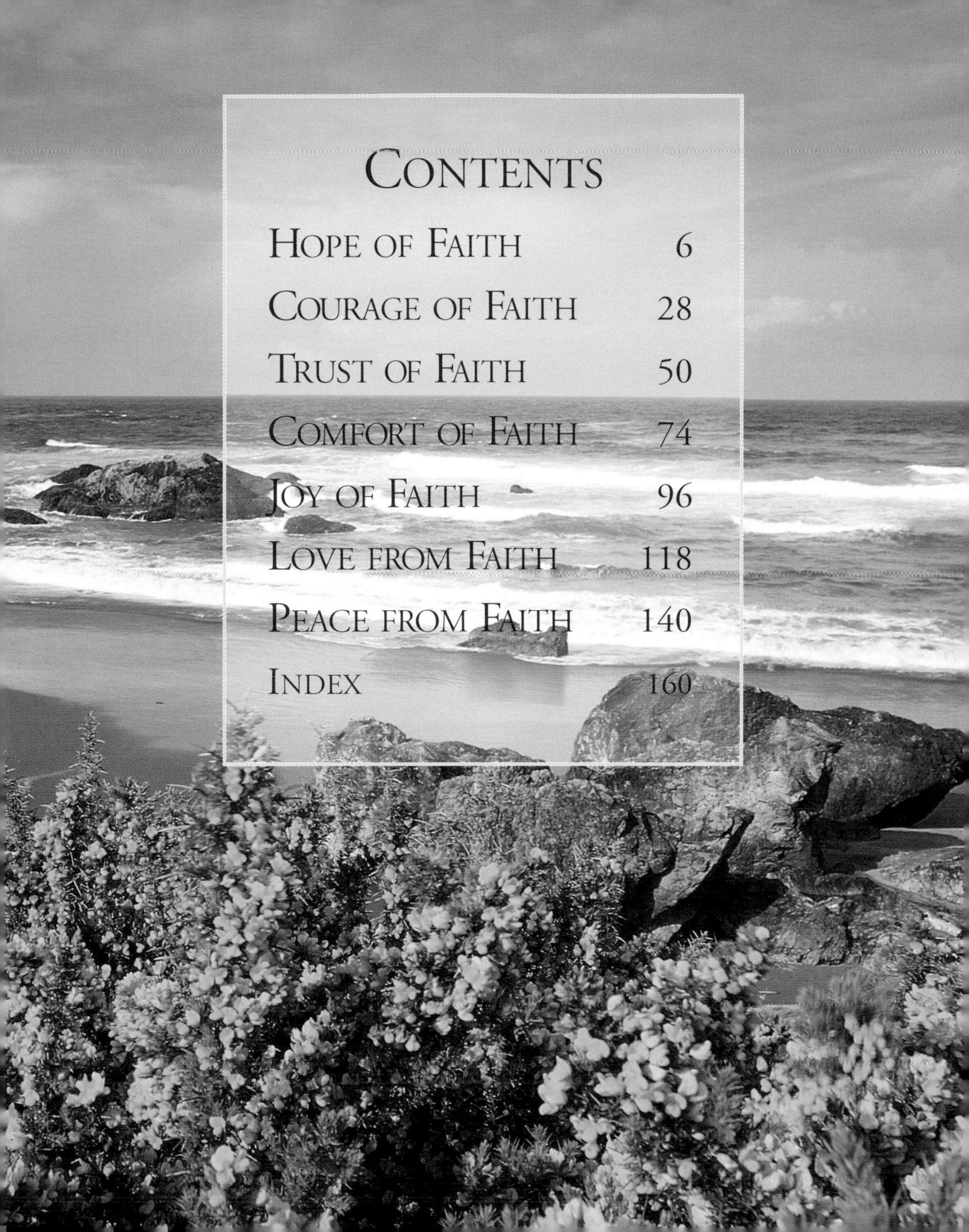

CONTENTS

HOPE OF FAITH   6

COURAGE OF FAITH   28

TRUST OF FAITH   50

COMFORT OF FAITH   74

JOY OF FAITH   96

LOVE FROM FAITH   118

PEACE FROM FAITH   140

INDEX   160

Chapter One

HOPE OF FAITH

Now the God of hope fill you with all joy and peace in believing, that ye may abound in hope, through the power of the Holy Ghost.
—ROMANS 15:13

The sun dips quietly behind the mountains near Peyto Lake in Banff National Park, Canada.

Daily Prayers Dissolve Your Cares

For thou art my hope, O Lord God: thou art my trust from my youth.

—Psalm 71:5

I meet God in the morning and go with Him through the day,
Then in the stillness of the night before sleep comes I pray
That God will just take over all the problems I can't solve;
And in the peacefulness of sleep my cares will all dissolve.

So when I open up my eyes to greet another day,
I'll find myself renewed in strength and there will open up a way
To meet what seemed impossible for me to solve alone;
And once again I'll be assured I am never on my own.

For there can be no failures or hopeless, unsaved sinners
If we enlist the help of God, who makes all losers winners.
So meet Him in the morning and go with Him through the day;
And thank Him for His guidance each evening when you pray.

And if you follow faithfully this daily way to pray,
You will never in your lifetime face another hopeless day.

Helen Steiner Rice

The Seventy-First Psalm

Lord, on Thee my trust is grounded;
Leave me not with shame confounded,
But in justice bring me aid.
Let Thine ear to me be bended;
Let my life from death defended
   Be by Thee in safety stayed.

Be my rock, my refuge tower;
Show Thy unresisted power
Working now Thy wonted will.
Thou, I say, that never feignest

In Thy biddings but remainest
   Still my rock, my refuge still.

O my God, my sole help-giver,
From this wicked me deliver,
From this wrongful, spiteful man,
In Thee trusting, on Thee standing,
With my childish understanding,
   Nay with life my hopes began.

Mary Sidney Herbert

Bandon Beach greets the morning sun in Oregon.

Blessed be the God and Father of our Lord Jesus Christ, which according to his abundant mercy hath begotten us again unto a lively hope by the resurrection of Jesus Christ from the dead.
—1 PETER 1:3

OUR ENDLESS HOME

May He give us
all the courage that we need
to go the way He shepherds us,

That when He calls
we may go unfrightened.

If He bids us come to Him
across the waters,
that unfrightened we may go.

And if He bids us climb a hill,
may we not notice that it is a hill,
mindful only of the happiness
of His company.

He made us for himself,
that we should travel with Him
and see Him at the last
in His unveiled beauty
in the abiding city where
He is light
and happiness
and endless home.

BEDE JARRETT

HOPE

This would I hold more precious than fine gold,
This would I keep although all else be lost:
Hope in the heart, that precious, priceless thing,
Hope at any cost.

And God, if its fine luster should be dimmed,
If seemingly through grief it may be spent,
Help me to wait without too much despair,
Too great astonishment.

Let me be patient when my spirit lacks
Its high exuberance, its shining wealth;
Hope is a matter, often, God, I know,
Of strength, of health.

Help me to wait until my strength returns,
Help me to climb each difficult, high slope;
Always within my heart some golden gleam,
Some quenchless spark of hope.

GRACE NOLL CROWELL

*A Douglas fir tree reaches
for the sky from Bryce Canyon
National Park, Utah.*

PRAYERS FOR HOPE

Lord, we thank Thee for that hour when the stone was rolled away, when sin and death had lost their power, and earth could sing that Easter Day—sing of Thy redemptive dying and the sacrifice it meant, sing of man's debt You paid, and Thy grace from Heaven sent.

Lord, we thank Thee that our groping through the centuries was finished, and the pardon for which we were hoping had, by Thee, been amply won. May we cease our futile striving and claim the grace that will suffice. We dedicate to Thee our living, knowing Thou hast paid the price.

ENID MARTELL OLSON

Almighty God, who has given Thine only Son to be unto us both a sacrifice for sin and also an example of Godly life, give us grace that we may always most thankfully receive His inestimable benefit, and also daily endeavor ourselves to follow the blessed steps of His most holy life; through the same Thy Son Jesus Christ our Lord. Amen.

AUTHOR UNKNOWN

Happy is he . . . whose hope is in the Lord his God.

—PSALM 146:5

O Thou who makest the stars and turnest the shadow of death into the morning, on this day of days we meet to render Thee, our Lord and King, the tribute of our praise—for the resurrection of our Lord Jesus Christ, for the new life of the springtime, for the sure triumph of truth, for the victory of light over darkness, for the everlasting hopes that rise within the human heart, and for the gospel which hath brought life and immortality to light. . . . Receive our thanksgiving, reveal Thy Presence, and send into our hearts the Spirit of the risen Christ.

AUTHOR UNKNOWN

O God, we thank Thee for the world in which Thou hast placed us, for the universe whose vastness is revealed in the blue depths of the sky, whose immensities are lit by shining stars beyond the strength of mind to follow. We thank Thee for every sacrament of beauty: for the sweetness of flowers, the solemnity of the stars, the sound of streams and swelling seas, for far-reaching lands and mighty mountains which rest and satisfy the soul, the purity of dawn which calls us to holy dedication, the peace of evening which speaks of everlasting rest.

WILLIAM E. ORCHARD

Almighty Father, who hast given Thine only Son to die for our sins and to rise again for our justification, grant us so to put away the leaven of malice and wickedness that we may always serve Thee in pureness of living and of truth; through the merits of the same Thy Son Jesus Christ our Lord. Amen.

BOOK OF COMMON PRAYER

O God, who never forsakest those that hope in Thee, grant that we may ever keep that hope which Thou hast given us by Thy Word as an anchor of our souls, to preserve us sure and steadfast, unshaken and secure in all the storms of life, through Jesus Christ our Lord.

AUTHOR UNKNOWN

O God, my Father, looking up at the shining stars of the cold, December sky, I remember the patient mother and the rock-hewn manger in lowly Bethlehem where lay cradled Thy Love for the world. In the shadows of the silent stall, I stand beside the Christ. Speak to my soul as I wait, I pray Thee. Let the trusting, loving spirit of the Child steal into my life until it calms my fears and soothes my pain. In willing surrender and passionate longing, let me take the Christ Child to my heart, that henceforth I may live as He lived, love as He loved, and, following His footsteps, bring help to the needy, courage to the weak, comfort to the sorrowing, and hope to the lost. Amen.

AUTHOR UNKNOWN

WE TRUST

Oh, yet we trust that somehow good
Will be the final goal of ill,
To pangs of nature, sins of will,
Defects of doubt, and taints of blood;

That nothing walks with aimless feet;
That not one life shall be destroyed
Or cast as rubbish to the void
When God hath made the pile complete;

That not a worm is cloven in vain;
That not a mouth with vain desire
Is shriveled in a fruitless fire
Or but subserves another's gain.

Behold, we know not anything;
I can but trust that good shall fall
At last—far off—at last, to all,
And every winter change to spring.

So runs my dream: but what am I?
An infant crying in the night,
An infant crying for the light,
And with no language but a cry.

I falter where I firmly trod,
And, falling with my weight of cares
Upon the great world's altar-stairs
That slope through darkness up to God,

I stretch lame hands of faith, and grope
And gather dust and chaff, and call
To what I feel is Lord of all
And faintly trust the larger hope.

ALFRED, LORD TENNYSON

HOPE DWELLS EVER IN THE SOUL

Life is never hopeless,
Never wholly without joy;
For Hope dwells ever in the soul,
And nothing can destroy
The power of Hope to rise again
In spite of tragedy. It can't be crushed
By circumstance or broken utterly.
Sometimes it may seem to fail
When Fortune strikes a blow.
We think our lives are ended,
Courage fades and faith burns low;
But ends are only new beginnings
Where we start again.
Much is taken with the years
But many things remain.

Bleak and bitter life may look
When we have suffered loss,
But there are consolations
In the shadow of the cross.
Sorrows come but not to stay;
The door is left ajar.
And every time a lamp goes out,
God lights another star.

PATIENCE STRONG

And now, Lord, what wait I for? my hope is in thee.

—PSALM 39:7

Lush greenery frames Oneonta Falls in Oregon.

What God Hath Promised

God hath not promised
Skies always blue,
Flower-strewn pathways
All our lives through;
God hath not promised
Sun without rain,
Joy without sorrow,
Peace without pain.

But God hath promised
Strength for the day,
Rest for the labor,
Light for the way,
Grace for the trials,
Help from above,
Unfailing sympathy,
Undying love.

ANNIE JOHNSON FLINT

Thy mercy, O Lord, is in the heavens; and thy faithfulness reacheth unto the clouds. How excellent is thy lovingkindness, O God! therefore the children of men put their trust under the shadow of thy wings.

—PSALM 36:5, 7

Spring bursts forth in the flowers and trees around this pond at Shore Acres State Park, Oregon.

THE SOLID ROCK

Edward Mote, 1797-1874

William B. Bradbury, 1816-1868

1. My hope is built on noth - ing less Than
2. When dark - ness veils His love - ly face, I
3. His oath, His cov - e - nant, His blood, Sup -
4. When He shall come with trum - pet sound, Oh,

Je - sus' blood and right - eous - ness; I dare not trust the
rest on His un - chang - ing grace; In ev - 'ry high and
port me in the whelm - ing flood; When all a - round my
may I then in Him be found; Dressed in His right - eous -

sweet - est frame, But whol - ly lean on Je - sus' name.
storm - y gale, My an - chor holds with - in the veil.
soul gives way, He then is all my hope and stay.
ness a - lone, Fault - less to stand be - fore the throne.

THE STREAM OF FAITH

From heart to heart, from creed to creed,
  The hidden river runs.
It quickens all the ages down;
  It binds the sires to sons—

The stream of Faith, whose source is God,
  Whose sound, the sound of prayer,
Whose meadows are the holy lives
  Upspringing everywhere.

And still it moves, a broadening flood,
  And fresher, fuller grows.
A sense as if the sea were near
  Toward which the river flows.

O Thou who art the secret Source
  That rises in each soul,
Thou art the Ocean, too, Thy charm,
  That ever-deepening roll!
WILLIAM CHANNING GANNETT

*I can do all things
through Christ which
strengtheneth me.*

—PHILIPPIANS 4:13

THE GRACE OF GOD

High in the heavens, eternal God,
  Thy goodness in full glory shines;
Thy truth shall break through every cloud
  That veils and darkens Thy designs.

Forever firm Thy justice stands,
  As mountains their foundations keep.
Wise are the wonders of Thy hands;
  Thy judgments are a mighty deep.

The Providence is kind and large;
  Both man and beast Thy bounty share.
The whole creation is Thy charge,
  But saints are Thy peculiar care.

My God, how excellent Thy grace,
  Whence all our hope and comfort springs!
The sons of Adam, in distress,
  Fly to the shadow of Thy wings.

From the provisions of Thy house
  We shall be fed with sweet repast;
There mercy like a river flows
  And brings salvation to our taste.

Life, like a fountain rich and free,
  Springs from the presence of my Lord;
And in Thy light our souls shall see
  The glories promised in Thy word.
ISAAC WATTS

Mount Bachelor, Oregon, rises from the beauty of autumn's colors.

SUN ON STONE

PATIENCE STRONG

Hope is like the sun upon the threshold of the heart. A glow lights up the inner room. The shadows fall apart; and rising to unlatch the door, we cast all fear away as we venture out into the brightness of the day.

Hope is like a ray of sunlight falling on gray stone. The heart is warmed. We're tempted out to take the road alone, out towards a broad horizon where the sky is gold with promise of the love of God and blessings manifold.

HOPE

Hope is a robin singing
On a rainy day;
He knows the sun will shine again
Though skies may now be gray.

Like the robin let us be,
Meet trouble with a smile;
And soon the sun will shine for us
In just a little while.

BEVERLY J. ANDERSON

GOD WILL DELIVER

SAINT FRANCIS DE SALES

Do not look forward to the changes and chances of this life in fear; rather look to them with full hope that as they arise, God, whose you are, will deliver you out of them. He has kept you hitherto—do you but hold fast to His dear hand, and He will lead you safely through all things; and, when you cannot stand, He will bear you in His arms. Do not look forward to what may happen tomorrow; the same everlasting Father who cares for you today will take care of you tomorrow and every day. Either He will shield you from suffering, or He will give you unfailing strength to bear it. Be at peace, then, and put aside all anxious thoughts and imaginations.

ASPECTS OF CHRISTIANITY

EPISTLE OF BARNABAS

There are three central aspects of Christianity. The first is the hope of eternal life, which is the beginning and end of our faith. The second is righteousness, which is the beginning and end of judgment. The third is joy, which is the beginning and end of love. Through the Resurrection of Jesus Christ, we have had a glimpse of what is promised for all who are saved because He is the first fruits of the harvest of salvation. Through the example of Jesus Christ in His life and work, we understand righteousness; and by following His example we can be sure of favorable judgment. Through the joy that Jesus mediates, which originates in His perfect heart of love, we want to share that joy and so grow in His love. Thus we need to hold fast to our hope, our righteousness, and our joy granted to us by God in Christ and finally rise to eternal life.

Let Israel hope in the Lord from henceforth and for ever.

—PSALM 131:3

Golden wheat fields stretch as far as the eye can see near Cortez, Colorado.

HOPE OF FAITH

23

EVIDENCE NOT SEEN

DARLENE DEIBLER ROSE

eace came to the Japanese prison camp at Kampili two weeks after it had been heralded in the high-roads and footpaths, the boulevards and cobbled tracks of the rest of the world. On September 19, 1945, seventeen days after the truce had been signed aboard the battleship USS *Missouri* in Tokyo Bay, I stepped carefully, balancing my emaciated eighty-pound frame, into a bobbing rowboat that was to carry me from Celebes, the island of my captivity, to a flying boat lying at anchor in the harbor sent to evacuate American personnel from the military prison camp.

Eight years before, and a war away, I had arrived in the islands with my husband on our first wedding anniversary to begin missionary work in the interior of New Guinea. Now, rowing away from the shore, I could think of nothing but two lonely wooden crosses, half-hidden on some remote hillside. One was the grave of the Reverend C. Russell Deibler, my husband; the other, that of Dr. Robert Alexander Jaffray, my spiritual mentor and an inimitable pioneer and visionary, who had given more than forty years in missionary service to China, Indochina, and Indonesia.

Now alone, I started the journey back to my homeland. How desolate the island shoreline seemed, despite the lush foliage and sparkling blue waters. I turned my face away as great bitterness corroded the edges of my soul like acid. Twenty-eight years old, already a widow for more than two years, I was returning to the United States without a single possession. My mementos and private keepsakes of married life had been pilfered or destroyed. I wore borrowed, ill-fitting clothes. A huge ulcer was eating into the flesh of one leg, and my once soft and fair skin was scarred and mottled from the hours I had spent working in the beastly tropical sun to advance the Japanese war effort. The diseases of imprisonment—beriberi, malaria, and dysentery—had left me frail and debilitated.

For almost four years, my fellow missionaries and I, along with 1,600 other women and children, measured our days in

Daisies line the coastline near Whale Cove, Oregon.

forced labor, meted the hours in separation and deprivation, and marked the anniversaries of the deaths of loved ones who succumbed, one by one, to disease, starvation, and the horrific bombings.

No other world had come to exist beyond the margins of a few barren acres for the hundreds of us incarcerated at Kampili. We were totally isolated; and the cataclysmic events that raged and scourged over the rest of the earth were interpreted to us solely through the eyes and whims of our Japanese captors.

Not a single letter arrived from home. Not one humane Red Cross package or one encouraging pamphlet was ever dropped by the Allies or ferreted under the barbed wire to assure us that someone was fighting for our freedom.

Now, suspended between captivity and a new life, I felt a fear I'd never known. Would I know how to live outside of the confined yet familiar regimen of suffering? Would I ever be free of the recurring, terrifying nightmares of trying to rescue people caught in burning buildings? . . . When would the mention of the Kempeitai Secret Police cease to fill me with terror? Or the sound of a plane not make me want to run and hide from the incendiary or shrapnel

bombs the plane surely carried? And when would seeing others delirious with joy at being reunited not constrict my heart, still aching with deep pain from my loss of Russell?

Suddenly I was awash in a sea of great bitterness. "Lord, I'll never come back to these islands again. They've robbed me of everything that was most dear to me." The rowboat reached the flying boat bound for intermediate stops in Borneo and the Palawan Island, then on to Manila. "Will there be healing for such hurt?" I could only cry out to God and hope. Healing would have to come if I were ever to truly live—whole and complete again.

Reaching up to grab the rope ladder dangling from the blister of the flying boat, a Catalina, I heard noises from the beach—running feet and calling voices. *Selamat djalan!* "A peaceful journey!" the Indonesian voices rang out across the distance. Those who had come to know the Lord in our Macassar Gospel Tabernacle and those who had shared in the indescribable suffering of imprisonment stood waving in a group. Notification of our departure had come so suddenly that I had been unable to say goodbye.

Their voices were raised in a sweet benediction: "God be with you, till we meet again. . . ." Their song released the waters of bitterness that had flooded my soul, and the hurt began to drain from me as my tears flowed in a steady stream. The healing had begun. I knew then that someday, God only knew when, I would come back to these my people and my island home.

As the Catalina became airborne, carrying me away from the bomb-scarred terrain, the flooded rice fields, the coral coastline, and the mountains of my long bondage, I handed over eight long years of my life into the faithful, wise hands of a gracious God Who alone could help me to understand the mysteries of deep pain and suffering.

The sun sets behind the palm trees at Launiupoko State Wayside in Maui, Hawaii.

Chapter Two
COURAGE OF FAITH

The Lord is my light and my salvation;
whom shall I fear? the Lord is the strength of
my life; of whom shall I be afraid?
—PSALM 27:1

The light of Yaquina Lighthouse in Oregon can still be
seen through the fog at sunrise.

THE LAMP OF FAITH

JAMES ALLEN

*W*here faith is, there is courage, there is fortitude, there is steadfastness and strength. . . . Faith bestows that sublime courage that rises superior to the troubles and disappointments of life, that acknowledges no defeat except as a step to victory, that is strong to endure, patient to wait, and energetic to struggle. . . . Light up, then, the lamp of faith in your heart. . . . It will lead you safely through the mists of doubt and the black darkness of despair, along the narrow, thorny ways of sickness and sorrow, and over the treacherous places of temptation and uncertainty.

BE STRONG

Be strong!
We are not here to play, to dream, to drift;
We have hard work to do and loads to lift;
Shun not the struggle—face it; 'tis God's gift.

Be strong!
Say not, "The days are evil. Who's to blame?"
And fold the hands and acquiesce—oh, shame!
Stand up, speak out, and bravely, in God's name.

Be strong!
It matters not how deep entrenched the wrong,
How hard the battle goes, the day how long;
Faint not—fight on! Tomorrow comes the song.

MALTBIE DAVENPORT BABCOCK

COURAGE

Riches I hold in light esteem
And Love I laugh to scorn;
And lust of Fame was but a dream
That vanished with the morn.

And if I pray, the only prayer
That moves my lips for me
Is "Leave the heart that now I bear
And give me liberty."

Yes, as my swift days near their goal,
'Tis all that I implore—
Through life and death a chainless soul,
With courage to endure!

EMILY BRONTË

Wait on the Lord: be of good courage,
and he shall strengthen thine heart.

—PSALM 27:14

A brilliant sunset at Boardman State Park, Oregon, brings the hope of a sunny tomorrow.

COURAGE OF FAITH

31

THE LORD'S LEADING

Thus far the Lord hath led us
　in darkness and in day,
Through all the varied stages
　of the narrow, homeward way.

Long since He took that journey
　He trod that path alone;
Its trials and its dangers
　full well Himself hath known.

Thus far the Lord hath led us;
　the promise hath not failed.
The enemy, encountered oft,
　has never quite prevailed.

The shield of faith has turned aside
　or quenched each fiery dart;
The Spirit's sword in weakest hands has
　forced him to depart.

Thus far the Lord hath led us;
　the waters have been high,
But yet in passing through them
　we felt that He was nigh.

A very present helper
　in trouble we have found;
His comforts most abounded
　when our sorrows did abound.

Thus far the Lord hath led us;
　and will He now forsake
The feeble ones whom for His own
　it pleases Him to take?

Oh, never, never! Earthly friends
　may cold and faithless prove,
But His is changeless pity
　and everlasting love.

Calmly we look behind us,
　our joys and sorrows past;
We know that all is mercy now
　and shall be well at last.

Calmly we look before us;
　we fear no future ill;
Enough for safety and for peace
　if Thou art with us still.

Author Unknown

Fear thou not; for I am with thee: be not dismayed; for I am thy God: I will strengthen thee; yea, I will help thee; yea, I will uphold thee with the right hand of my righteousness.

—Isaiah 41:10

Brilliant colors of autumn stand out through the fog along Aufderheide National Scenic Byway, Willamette National Forest, Oregon.

THE IDEALS TREASURY OF FAITH AND INSPIRATION

32

Prayers for Courage

May we who are pilgrims, conscious of life's varying scenes, learn by faith, our Father, to cling to Thee. We know that Thou wilt be in the future as Thou has been in the past. We know that Thou wilt lead us on through all the tomorrows as Thou hast led us through the yesterdays. We know that Thou wilt not let us go, even when we, in willful neglect and indulgence, try to wander from Thy way. As we set our faces toward the new year, we know full well that it will bring many changes. The old must give place to the new. Time does not stand still, nor the world cease from its turning. Wilt Thou give to us the courage and fortitude of mature men and women that will enable us to stand upon our faith, as the spirit of the living Lord shall give us strength. In Thy strong name we pray. Amen.

Peter Marshall

God make me brave for Life—oh, braver than this!
Let me straighten after pain as a tree straightens
after the rain, shining and lovely again.

God make me brave for Life—much braver than
this! As the blown glass lifts, let me rise from sorrow with quiet eyes, knowing Thy way is wise.

God make me brave—life brings such blinding
things. Help me to keep my sight; help me to see
aright that out of the dark comes Light.

Grace Noll Crowell

Grant me, O Lord, the royalty of inward happiness and the serenity which comes from living close to Thee. Daily renew in me the sense of joy, and let the eternal spirit of the Father dwell in my soul and body, filling every corner of my heart with light and grace; so that, bearing about with me the infection of a good courage, I may be a diffuser of life and may meet all ills and cross accidents with gallant and high-hearted courage, giving Thee thanks always for all things. Amen.

Author Unknown

Give us courage, O Lord, to stand up and be counted; to stand up for others who cannot stand up for themselves; to stand up for ourselves when it is needful to do so.

Let us fear nothing more than we fear Thee.

Let us love nothing more than we love Thee, for then we shall fear nothing also.

Let us have no other god before Thee, whether nation or party or state or church. Let us seek no other peace but the peace which is Thine; and make us its instruments, opening our eyes and our ears and our hearts, so that we should know always what work of peace we should do for Thee.

ALAN PATON

Be strong and of good courage . . . fear not, nor be dismayed: for the Lord God, even my God, will be with thee; he will not fail thee, nor forsake thee . . .

—1 CHRONICLES 28:20

Give us, O Lord, a steadfast heart, which no unworthy affection may drag down; give us an unconquered heart, which no tribulation can wear out; give us an upright heart, which no unworthy purpose may tempt aside. Bestow upon us also, O Lord our God, understanding to know Thee, diligence to seek Thee, wisdom to find Thee, and a faithfulness that may finally embrace Thee, even through Jesus Christ our Lord.

THOMAS AQUINAS

Almighty God, Lord of the storm and of the calm, the vexed sea and quiet haven, of day and night, of life and of death; grant unto us so to have our hearts stayed upon Thy faithfulness, Thine unchangingness and love, that, whatsoever betide us, however black the cloud or dark the night, with quiet faith trusting in Thee with untroubled eye, and walking in lowliness toward Thee and in lovingness toward one another, abide all storms and troubles of this mortal life, beseeching Thee that they may turn to the soul's true good; we ask it for Thy mercy's sake, shown in Jesus Christ our Lord. Amen.

GEORGE DAWSON

I do not ask to walk smooth paths nor bear an easy load. I pray for strength and fortitude to climb the rock-strewn road.

Give me such courage; I can scale the hardest peaks alone and transform every stumbling block into a stepping stone.

GAIL BROOK BURKET

A Psalm of Life

Tell me not in mournful numbers,
    "Life is but an empty dream!"
For the soul is dead that slumbers,
    And things are not what they seem.

Life is real! Life is earnest!
    And the grave is not its goal;
"Dust thou art, to dust returnest,"
    Was not spoken of the soul.

Not enjoyment and not sorrow
    Is our destined end or way
But to act, that each tomorrow
    Find us farther than today.

Art is long, and time is fleeting,
    And our hearts, though stout and brave,
Still, like muffled drums, are beating
    Funeral marches to the grave.

In the world's broad field of battle,
    In the bivouac of life,

Be not like dumb, driven cattle!
    Be a hero in the strife!

Trust no future, howe'er pleasant!
    Let the dead past bury its dead!
Act, act in the living present!
    Heart within and God o'erhead!

Lives of great men all remind us
    We can make our lives sublime,
And, departing, leave behind us
    Footprints on the sands of time.

Footprints, that perhaps another,
    Sailing o'er life's solemn main,
A forlorn and shipwrecked brother,
    Seeing, shall take heart again.

Let us, then, be up and doing,
    With a heart for any fate;
Still achieving, still pursuing,
    Learn to labor and to wait.

Henry Wadsworth Longfellow

A Life Heroic

I like the man who faces what he must
With step triumphant and a heart of cheer,
Who fights the daily battle without fear;
Sees his hopes fail, yet keeps unfaltering trust
That God is God; that somehow, true and just
His plans work out for mortals; not a tear
Is shed when fortune, which the world
    holds dear,
Falls from his grasp; better, with love, a crust
Than living in dishonor; envies not
Nor loses faith in man but does his best;
Nor ever mourns over his humbler lot,
But with a smile and words of hope, gives zest
To every toiler; he alone is great
Who by a life heroic conquers fate.

Sarah K. Bolton

Big leaf maple leaves swirl in North Fork Silver Creek in Silver Falls State Park, Oregon.

Courage of Faith

Storm clouds gather over the painted hills that rise above John Day Fossil Beds National Monument, Oregon.

THREE LESSONS

There are three lessons I would write,
Three words, as with a golden pen,
In tracings of eternal light
Upon the hearts of men.

Have hope! Though clouds environ round
And gladness hides her face in scorn,
Put thou the shadow from thy brow;
No night but has its morn.

Have faith! Where'er thy bark is driven,
The calm's disport, the tempest's mirth.

Know this: God rules the hosts of heaven,
The inhabitants of earth.

Have love! Not love alone for one,
But man as man thy brother call,
And scatter, like the circling sun,
Thy charities on all.

Thus grave these words upon thy soul:
Hope, faith, and love. And thou shalt find
Strength when life's surges maddest roll,
Light when thou else were blind.

Johann Christoph Friedrich von Schiller

Do Not Worry about Your Life

Dietrich Bonhoeffer

We used to think that one of the inalienable rights of man was that he should be able to plan both his professional and his private life. That is a thing of the past. The force of circumstances has brought us into a situation where we have to give up being "anxious about tomorrows" (Matthew 6:34). But it makes all the difference whether we accept this willingly and in faith (as the Sermon on the Mount intends) or under continual constraint.

For most people, the compulsory abandonment of planning for the future means that they are forced back into living just for the moment, irresponsibly, frivolously, or resignedly; some few dream longingly of better times to come and try to forget the present. We find both these courses equally impossible, and there remains for us only the very narrow way, often extremely difficult to find, of living every day as if it were our last, and yet living in faith and responsibility as though there were to be a great future: "Houses and fields and vineyards shall be possessed again in this land," proclaims Jeremiah (32:15), in paradoxical contrast to his prophecies of woe, just before the destruction of the holy city.

It is a sign from God and a pledge of a fresh start and a great future just when all seems black. Thinking and acting for the sake of the coming generation, but being ready to go any day without fear or anxiety—that, in practice, is the spirit in which we are forced to live. It is not easy to be brave and keep the spirit alive, but it is imperative.

Take therefore no thought for the morrow: for the morrow shall take thought for the things of itself.

—Matthew 6:34

A MIGHTY FORTRESS IS OUR GOD

Martin Luther, 1483-1546
Trans. Frederick H. Hedge, 1805-1890

Martin Luther, 1483-1546

1. A mighty fortress is our God, A bulwark never failing; Our helper He, amid the flood Of mortal ills prevailing.
2. Did we in our own strength confide, Our striving would be losing, Were not the right Man on our side, The Man of God's own choosing.
3. And though this world, with devils filled, Should threaten to undo us, We will not fear, for God hath willed His truth to triumph through us.
4. That word above all earthly powers— No thanks to them— abideth; The Spirit and the gifts are ours Through Him Who with us sideth.

For still our an-cient foe Doth seek to work us
Dost ask who that may be? Christ Je-sus, it is
The prince of dark-ness grim— We trem-ble not for
Let goods and kin-dred go, This mor-tal life, al-

woe; His craft and pow'r are great, And, armed with cru-el
He; Lord Sab-a-oth His name, From age to age the
him; His rage we can en-dure, For lo, his doom is
so; The bod-y they may kill: God's truth a-bid-eth

hate, On earth is not his e - qual.
same, And He must win the bat - tle.
sure, One lit-tle word shall fell - him.
still, His King-dom is for-ev - er.

FINDING HAPPINESS

ANNE FRANK

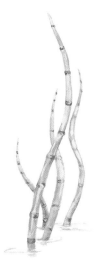

hen I looked outside right into the depth of Nature and God, then I was happy, really happy. . . .

Riches can all be lost, but that happiness in your own heart can only be veiled, and it will still bring you happiness again, as long as you live. As long as you can look fearlessly up into the heavens, as long as you know that you are pure within, and that you will still find happiness. *February 23, 1944*

I've found that there is always some beauty left—in nature, sunshine, freedom, in yourself; these can all help you. Look at these things, then you find yourself again, and God, and then you regain your balance. And whoever is happy will make others happy too. He who has courage and faith will never perish in misery! *March 7, 1944*

PSALM TWENTY-THREE

The Lord is my shepherd; I shall not want.
He maketh me to lie down in green pastures:
He leadeth me beside the still waters.
He restoreth my soul:
He leadeth me in the paths of righteousness for his name's sake.
Yea, though I walk through the valley of the shadow of death,
I will fear no evil: for thou art with me;
Thy rod and thy staff they comfort me.
Thou preparest a table before me in the presence of mine enemies:
Thou anointest my head with oil; my cup runneth over.

Surely goodness and mercy
Shall follow me all the days of my life:
And I will dwell in the house of the Lord for ever.

The beauty of God's earth abounds at Punchbowl Falls in Oregon.

Like a Candle

Like a candle in the night
The Word of God illumines me,
Till out of darkness into light
I walk as one who now can see.

And, seeing, I am not afraid;
For what is there on earth to fear
Since all is good that God has made,
And God Himself is ever near?

Marie Barton

Courage

When weeping stopped, I saw the earth was green.
I found that hearts can heal and throb again,
That morning's sky is evening's opaline.
When weeping stopped and there was no more pain,
I found that life can sing a glad refrain.

With shoulders straight, I scaled the steep ascent,
Crag after crag, forgetful of the force
Below. With shining eyes, I knew content.
My cup is full. My lips can frame a song.
I will go on. I shall be tall and strong.

Mabel Demers Hinckley

He Leads Me On

Oh, this I know—though shadows deep fall o'er me,
And though the road be rough and dark and long,
My Master walked the selfsame way before me,
And so I journey with a song.
I journey onward with a song!

The winds blow cold and angry storms assail me,
And heart grows faint and strength is almost gone;
The sunshine of His love will never fail me,
The night of pain departs with dawn.
The pain departs with glorious dawn!

I see His footprints on the road to glory;
They point the way to glad and great release.
I hear the angels sing the wondrous story;
My heart grows strong and filled with peace.
My soul is filled with His sweet peace!

June Palmerston

Be strong and of a good courage; be not afraid, neither be thou dismayed: for the Lord thy God is with thee whithersoever thou goest.

—Joshua 1:9

Clouds partially obscure the Snake River and the peaks of the Grand Tetons at Teton National Park, Wyoming.

CHRIST WITH ME, CHRIST BEFORE ME

Christ to protect me today
    against poison, against burning,
    against drowning, against wounding,
    so that there may come abundance of reward.
Christ with me, Christ before me, Christ behind me,
Christ in me, Christ beneath me, Christ above me,
Christ on my right, Christ on my left,
Christ where I lie, Christ where I sit, Christ where I arise,
Christ in the heart of every man who thinks of me,
Christ in the mouth of every man who speaks of me,
Christ in every eye that sees me,
Christ in every ear that hears me.

SAINT PATRICK

...for he hath said, I will never leave thee, nor forsake thee.

—HEBREWS 13:5

FOOTPRINTS

One night I dreamed a dream.
I was walking along the beach with my Lord.
Across the dark sky flashed scenes from my life.
For each scene, I noticed two sets
of footprints in the sand,
one belonging to me
and one to my Lord.
When the last scene of my life shot before me,
I looked back at the footprints in the sand.
There was only one set of footprints.
I realized that this was at the lowest
and saddest times of my life.
This always bothered me
and I questioned the Lord
about my dilemma.
"Lord, you told me when I decided to follow You,
You would walk and talk with me all the way.
But I'm aware that during the most troublesome
times of my life there is only one set of footprints.
I just don't understand why, when I needed You most,
You left me."
He whispered, "My precious child,
I love you and will never leave you,
never, ever, during your trials and testings.
When you saw only one set of footprints,
it was then that I carried you."

MARGARET FISHBACK POWERS

With Harney Lake in the distance, the wind has left its trail on the sand dunes of Malheur National Wildlife Refuge, Oregon.

SMALL GRACES

TERRY ANDERSON

t the time it was a mystery. Why was I led to that old church? It had happened in the fall of 1984 when my fiancée, Madeleine, and I were visiting her family in Sunderland, a town in northern England. I had looked forward to peace and quiet, a respite from my hectic career. . . . I had joined the Associated Press, reporting disasters, plane hijacks, rebellions, and, for the past several years, covering the ongoing violence in Lebanon.

I was so dispirited that it took me some days to settle down, even in the pleasant atmosphere of this English hamlet. As we strolled its neat streets, inhaling the crisp, early winter air, I noticed a church steeple outlined against the pale blue sky. Although I had been brought up in the Catholic church back in Batavia, New York, I had drifted far from God and considered myself an agnostic. Why did that tall, gray spire keep catching my eye?

After a few days in Sunderland, I finally decided to walk over to the church. When I got there I pulled open the heavy, oaken door, stepped in and settled in a worn pew. Looking up at the altar and

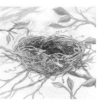

cross gleaming in the shadows, I suddenly had a strong sense of coming home. This was where I belonged. I believed in God the Father, His Son, Christ Jesus, and His Holy Spirit.

For the next six months back at work I tried to sort through this revelation. What did it mean in my life? What was I required to do? I was beginning to sense a closer relationship with God when, one morning on a street in Beirut, I was shoved at gunpoint into the back of a green Mercedes. My face was pressed to the floor and a blanket thrown over me as the car accelerated. It was March 16, 1985.

I lay on a cot for twenty-four days, eyes covered by a blindfold, chains painfully tight on my wrists and ankles. Finally, as shoes scraped the floor nearby, I gasped in Arabic, "Hey, chebab" ("mister").

The footsteps halted.

"You can't do this to me," I said. "I'm a man, not an animal. I'll go crazy."

"What do you want?"

"A Bible."

He left without another word. The next day something thudded on my cot. My chains were loosened; I sat up. The blindfold was removed, but the blanket was pulled over my head so that I couldn't see anything except the book on my lap.

It was a Bible, the Revised Standard Version, red cover.

In the past, I had read parts of the Bible on an intellectual level. Now I scoured its pages, book by book. I read it through, ten times, twenty, fifty. Each time, I found something new to sustain me. . . .

Amid the filth, the beatings, and the chains that shackled me to a wall, I felt so close to the long-suffering Job. I cried out to God with him: "I'm a good man. Why are You doing this to me? It's not fair!"

God answered: It doesn't have to be fair. I'm going to do what I want and you have to accept it. So it was that I began to learn acceptance. . . .

Months and then years ground on, each dismal day a dull blur of boredom, punctuated by cruelty, bad food, and sickness. Most torturous of all was the deep aching I felt for my family and loved ones.

My captors moved me from one secret location to another, wrapped like a mummy head to toe in plastic tape, with only my nostrils exposed. I was transported in a car trunk or, worse, in a hidden compartment under a truck. As we bumped along potholed pavements, exhaust fumes filled the narrow compartment, burning my nostrils; I was overcome with nausea, and struggled to keep from throwing up. I calmed myself with the rosary's hypnotic repetition: "Hail Mary, full of grace . . ."

When I learned of my father's death, and then my brother's, I could only pray with David: "Why hast thou forsaken me? Why art thou so far from helping me, from the words of my groaning?" (Psalm 22:1, RSV).

Again and again amid our grinding ordeal, small graces came. Among the hostages was Father Martin Jenko. We conducted worship services twice a day in what we called the Church of the Locked Door.

In a moment of darkness, I prayed for hope. My guard brought me a newspaper. It carried a photo of some schoolchildren presenting my sister, Peggy, a birthday card they had made for me. The glimpse of those children was a great comfort.

After almost seven years came my day of release: December 4, 1991. Reporters asked if I could ever forgive my captors. I hesitated a moment but then I answered, "Yes, as a Christian I am required to forgive, no matter how hard it may be."

I learned so much in those 2,455 days. I don't know what lies ahead, but whenever I need to know where my help will come from, I will recall an old church in an English town, and a worn red Bible. And I will remember what Joseph said in forgiving his brothers who had sold him into captivity: "You meant evil against me; but God meant it for good" (Genesis 50:20, RSV).

Chapter Three

TRUST OF FAITH

The Lord is my rock, and my fortress, and my deliverer; my God, my strength, in whom I will trust.

—PSALM 18:2

Saving Faith through Trust

Charles Spurgeon

Faith has specially to believe in Him who is the sum and substance of all this revelation, even Jesus Christ, who became God in human flesh that He might redeem our fallen nature from all the evils of sin and raise it to eternal felicity. We believe in Christ, on Christ, and upon Christ; accepting Him because of the record which God has given to us concerning His Son—that He is the propitiation for our sins. We accept God's unspeakable gift and receive Jesus as our all in all.

If I wanted to describe saving faith in one word, I should say that it is trust. It is so believing God and so believing in Christ that we trust ourselves and our eternal destinies in the hands of a reconciled God.

. . . the just shall live by his faith.

—Habakkuk 2:4

Father, Take My Hand

My Father, take my hand, for I am prone
To danger, and I fear to go alone.
I trust Thy guidance. Father, take my hand;
Lead Thy child safely through the desert land.
The way is dark before me; take my hand,
For light can only come at Thy command.
Clinging to Thy dear love, no doubt I know
That love will cheer my way where'er I go.
Father, the storm is breaking o'er me wild;
I feel its bitterness; protect Thy child.

The tempest-clouds are flying through the air;
Oh, take my hand and save me from despair.
Father, as I ascend the craggy steep
That leads me to Thy temple, let me keep
My hand in Thine, so I can conquer time
And by Thine aiding to Thy bosom climb.
Father, I feel the damp upon my brow,
The chill of death is falling on me now.
Soon from earth's flitting shadows I must part.
My Father, take my hand; Thou hast my heart.

Samuel Dowse Robbins

I waited patiently for the Lord; and he inclined unto me, and heard my cry. And he hath put a new song in my mouth, even praise unto our God: many shall see it, and fear, and shall trust in the Lord.

—PSALM 40:1, 3

HE KEEPS THE KEY

Is there some problem in your life to solve,
   Some passage seeming full of mystery?
God knows, who brings the hidden things to light.
   He keeps the key.

Is there some door closed by the Father's hand
   Which widely opened you had hoped to see?
Trust God and wait—for when He shuts the door,
   He keeps the key.

Is there some earnest prayer unanswered yet,
   Or answered not as you had thought 'twould be?
God will make clear His purpose by-and-by.
   He keeps the key.

Have patience with your God, your patient God,
   All wise, all knowing, no long tarrier He;
And of the door of all thy future life,
   He keeps the key.

Unfailing comfort, sweet and blessed rest,
   To know of every door He keeps the key,
That He at last, when just He sees 'tis best,
   Will give the key to Thee.

AUTHOR UNKNOWN

LIGHT SHINING OUT OF DARKNESS

God moves in a mysterious way,
His wonders to perform;
He plants His footsteps in the sea;
He rides upon the storm.

Ye fearful saints, fresh courage take,
The clouds ye so much dread
Are big with mercy and shall break
In blessings on your head.

Judge not the Lord by feeble sense,
But trust Him for His grace.
Behind a frowning providence
He hides a smiling face.

His purposes will ripen fast,
Unfolding every hour;
The bud may have a bitter taste,
But sweet will be the flower.

Blind unbelief is sure to err
And scan His work in vain;
God is His own interpreter,
And He will make it plain.

WILLIAM COWPER

A storm at sea sends the waves crashing at Shore Acres State Park on Oregon's coast.

PRAYERS

OF

TRUST

Almighty God, Father of all mercies, we give Thee most humble and hearty thanks for all Thy goodness and loving kindness to us and to all men. We bless Thee for our creation, preservation, and all the blessings of this life; but above all, for Thine inestimable love in the redemption of the world by our Lord Jesus Christ; for the means of grace, and for the hope of glory. And, we beseech Thee, give us that due sense of all Thy mercies, that our hearts may be unfeignedly thankful; and that we show forth Thy praise, not only with our lips, but in our lives, by giving up ourselves to Thy service, and by walking before Thee in holiness through Jesus Christ our Lord, to whom, with Thee and the Holy Ghost, be all honor and glory, world without end. Amen.

AUTHOR UNKNOWN

Give me patience with life, so that I may not give up hope when hopes are long in coming true; so that I may accept disappointment without bitterness and delay without complaint.

WILLIAM BARCLAY

O Father, I will trust Thee: for all the known and all the unknown good that I have ever had has come from Thee. Sweet Saviour, I will trust Thee: Thy grace is all-sufficient for my soul, as mighty as Thy power and as matchless as Thy love. Blest Spirit, I will trust Thee: how can I ever dare to trust myself, to think, or speak, or act apart from Thee? O God, my God, my hope and stay, who knowest and orderest all that is best, I know not what to will or do aright; then make me ever love to choose and do Thy will.

WALTER HOWARD FRERE

Lord, increase our faith. We believe; help Thou our unbelief. Give us a true child's trust in Thee, in all Thy strength and goodness. Cause us to rest in perfect confidence in all Thy purposes and ways. Enable us to confide all our interests for time and for eternity to Thy keeping. Give us, heavenly Father, the substance of things hoped for and the evidence of things unseen, that we may walk by faith, not by sight, looking not at the things which are seen and temporal but at those things which are not seen and eternal.

AUTHOR UNKNOWN

Stand by me, You true Eternal God! In no man do I trust. Stand by me, O God, in the name of Your dear Son Jesus Christ, who shall be my defense and shelter, yes, my mighty fortress, through all the might and strength of Your Holy Spirit. Amen.

MARTIN LUTHER

May our Saviour Jesus Christ be with us wherever we go and may the spirit of Christmas warm our hearts all year long. May the selfsame spirit of love that bore our sins and led to our forgiveness reside in us. May we grow in the grace and peace of the Child of Bethlehem. Amen.

AUTHOR UNKNOWN

The God of my rock; in him will I trust: he is my shield, and the horn of my salvation, my high tower, and my refuge, my saviour. . . .

—2 SAMUEL 22:3

O Lord, Thou knowest that which is best for us; let this or that be done, as Thou shalt please. Give what Thou wilt, how much Thou wilt, and when Thou wilt. Deal with me as Thou thinkest best. Place me where Thou wilt, and deal with me in all things just as Thou wilt. Behold, I am Thy servant, prepared for all things: I desire not to live unto myself but unto Thee; and oh, that I could do it worthily and perfectly!

THOMAS À KEMPIS

GOD KNOWS

God knows—not I—the devious way
Wherein my faltering feet may tread
Before, into the light of day,
My steps from out this gloom are led.
And since my Lord the path doth see,
What matter if 'tis hid from me?

God knows—not I—how sweet accord
Shall grow at length from out this clash
Of earthly discords which have jarred
On soul and sense; I hear the crash,
Yet feel and know that on His ear
Breaks harmony—full, deep, and clear.

God knows—not I—why, when I'd fain
Have walked in pastures green and fair,
The path He pointed me hath lain
Through rocky deserts, bleak and bare.
I blindly trust—since 'tis His will—
This way lies safety, that way ill.

He knoweth too, despite my will,
I'm weak when I should be most strong.
And after earnest wrestling still
I see the right yet do the wrong.
Is it that I may learn at length
Not mine but His, the saving strength?

His perfect plan I may not grasp,
Yet I can trust Love Infinite,
And with my feeble fingers clasp
The hand that leads me into light.
My soul upon His errands goes,
The end I know not—but God knows.

AUTHOR UNKNOWN

The eerie light of an approaching storm accentuates the meadow grass in Jorden Valley, Oregon.

Behold, God is my salvation;
I will trust, and not be afraid: for the
Lord Jehovah is my strength and my
song; he also is become my salvation.
—ISAIAH 12:2

Trust in the Lord with
all thine heart; and lean
not unto thine own
understanding.
—PROVERBS 3:5

WHEN IS THE TIME TO TRUST?

When is the time to trust?
Is it when all is calm,
When waves the victor's palm,
And life is one glad psalm
Of joy and praise?

Nay! but the time to trust
Is when the waves beat high,
When storm clouds fill the sky,
And prayer is one long cry,
Oh, help and save!

When is the time to trust?
Is it when friends are true?
Is it when comforts woo,
And in all we say and do
We meet but praise?

Nay! but the time to trust
Is when we stand alone,
And summer birds have flown,
And every drop is gone,
All else but God.

What is the time to trust?
Is it some future day,
When you have tried your way,
And learned to trust and pray
By bitter woe?

Nay! but the time to trust
Is in this moment's need,
Poor, broken, bruised reed!
Poor, troubled soul, make speed
To trust thy God.

What is the time to trust?
Is it when hopes beat high,
When sunshine gilds the sky,
And joy and ecstasy
Fill all the heart?

Nay! but the time to trust
Is when our joy is fled,
When sorrow bows the head,
And all is cold and dead,
All else but God.

AUTHOR UNKNOWN

Fog and mist shroud the lower falls on the Yellowstone River in Wyoming.

TRUST

THOMAS À KEMPIS

*H*umility and patience in adversity more please Me, My son, than much comfort and devotion in prosperity. And why should a little thing spoken against thee make thee sad? Had it been greater, thou shouldst not have been disturbed. But now let it pass: 'tis nothing strange; it hath happed before; and if thou live longer, it will happen again.

Consider thy great weakness, which thou discoverest often in trifling concerns; and yet it is all for thy good, when these or such like things befall thee. Put the matter as well as thou canst out of thy mind; and if the tribulation hath touched thee, let it not cast thee down nor entangle thee.

The storm that hath arisen will quickly subside; and thy hidden pain will be soothed by returning grace.

I still Am, saith the Lord, ready to aid thee and console thee more than ever, if thou but trust Me, and beseech Me with all thy heart.

Be more tranquil in mind, and brace thyself to better fortitude;

All is not lost, even though again and again thou feel thyself broken or well-nigh spent.

'TIS SO SWEET TO TRUST IN JESUS

Louisa M. R. Stead, 1850-1917

William J. Kirkpatrick, 1838-1921

1. 'Tis so sweet to trust in Je - sus,
2. O how sweet to trust in Je - sus,
3. Yes, 'tis sweet to trust in Je - sus,
4. I'm so glad I learned to trust Thee,

Just to take Him at His Word; Just to rest up -
Just to trust His cleans - ing blood; Just in sim - ple
Just from sin and self to cease; Just from Je - sus
Pre - cious Je - sus, Sav - ior, Friend; And I know that

on His prom - ise; Just to know, "Thus saith the Lord."
faith to plunge me 'Neath the heal - ing, cleans - ing flood!
sim - ply tak - ing Life and rest, and joy, and peace.
Thou art with me, Wilt be with me to the end.

Broken Top Mountain is reflected in the lake below at Three Sisters' Wilderness, Oregon.

THE FAITH OF A MARINER

CHARLES SPURGEON

*L*ook at the faith of the master mariner! I have often wondered at it. He looses his cable—he steams away from the land. For days, weeks, or even months he sees neither sail nor shore; yet on he goes day and night without fear, till one morning he finds himself exactly opposite to the desired haven toward which he has been steering. How has he found his way over the trackless deep? He has trusted in his compass, his nautical almanac, his glass, and the heavenly bodies; and, obeying their guidance, without sighting land, he has steered so accurately that he has not to change a point to enter into port. It is a wonderful thing—that sailing or steaming without sight. Spiritually it is a blessed thing to leave altogether the shores of sight and feeling and to say "good-bye" to inward feelings, cheering providences, signs, tokens, and so forth. It is glorious to be far out on the ocean of divine love, believing in God, and steering for Heaven straight away by the direction of the Word of God.

Look on the Sunny Side

There are always two sides,
  the good and the bad,
The dark and the light,
  the sad and the glad.

But in looking back over
  the good and the bad,
We're aware of the number
  of good things we've had.

So thank God for good things
  He has already done;
And be grateful to Him
  for the battles you've won,

And know that the same God
  who helped you before
Is ready and willing
  to help you once more.

Then with faith in your heart
  reach out for God's Hand
And accept what He sends,
  though you can't understand—

For Our Father in Heaven
  always knows what is best,
And if you trust in His wisdom,
  your life will be blest.

Helen Steiner Rice

*Then shall ye call upon me,
and ye shall go and pray unto
me, and I will hearken unto
you. And ye shall seek me, and
find me, when ye shall search for
me with all your heart.*

—Jeremiah 29:12–13

Prayer

I asked for bread; God gave me a stone instead.
Yet while I pillowed there my weary head,
The angels made a ladder of my dreams,
Which upward to celestial mountains led.
And when I woke beneath the morning's beams,
Around my resting place fresh manna lay;
And, praising God, I went upon my way
  For I was fed.

God answers prayer; sometimes, when hearts are weak,
He gives the very gifts believers seek.
But often faith must learn a deeper rest
And trust God's silence when He does not speak.
For He whose name is Love will send the best.
Stars may burn out, nor mountain walls endure,
But God is true. His promises are sure
  For those who seek.

Author Unknown

HEROES OF FAITH

HEBREWS 11:2–4, 6–10, 13–16

For by it the elders obtained a good report. Through faith we understand that the worlds were framed by the word of God, so that things which are seen were not made of things which do appear. By faith Abel offered unto God a more excellent sacrifice than Cain, by which he obtained witness that he was righteous, God testifying of his gifts. . . . But without faith it is impossible to please him: for he that cometh to God must believe that he is, and that he is a rewarder of them that diligently seek him. By faith Noah, being warned of God of things not seen as yet, moved with fear, prepared an ark to the saving of his house; by the which he condemned the world, and became heir of the righteousness which is by faith. By faith Abraham, when he was called to go out into a place which he should afterward receive for an inheritance, obeyed; and he went out, not knowing whither he went. By faith he sojourned in the land of promise, as in a strange country, dwelling in tabernacles with Isaac and Jacob, the heirs with him of the same promise: For he looked for a city which hath foundations, whose builder and maker is God.

These all died in faith, not having received the promises, but having seen them afar off, and were persuaded of them, and embraced them, and confessed that they were strangers and pilgrims on the earth. For they that say such things declare plainly that they seek a country. And truly, if they had been mindful of that country from whence they came out, they might have had opportunity to have returned. But now they desire a better country, that is, an heavenly:

Wherefore God is not ashamed to be called their God: for he hath prepared for them a city.

Faith is the substance of things hoped for, the evidence of things not seen.

—HEBREWS 11:1

I BELIEVE

I believe.
That is to say,
The lenses of my soul sweep Heaven alway.

I believe.
By this I mean
My mind is open to the things unseen.

I believe.
I firmly hold
To untimed truth that never has been told.

I believe
What has been told
By men of worth, whom years do not make old.

I believe
Judea's Son,
Whose work continues, as it had begun.

I believe
Tomorrow's Light
Is always burning round the rim of night.

J. B. LAWRENCE

The living, the living, he shall praise thee, as I do this day: the father to the children shall make known thy truth.

—ISAIAH 38:19

*The moon rises over Lost Lake
with Mount Hood, Oregon,
in the background.*

How We Bought L'Abri

Edith Schaeffer

*S*uddenly I began to pray. . . . Suddenly, in the midst of my prayer, I felt a surge of faith in the God of Elijah, Daniel, and Joseph. I prayed: "But God, if You want us to stay in Switzerland, if Your word to me concerning L'Abri means our being in these mountains, then I know You are able to find a house, and lead me to it in the next half hour. Nothing is impossible to You. But You will have to do it. I can't even talk to anyone without breaking down."

I went down towards the main street of Villars just as a chattering, laughing crowd was coming back from skiing, crowding into the tearooms.

Walking through the lighthearted crowd I kept my eyes down on the snowy pavement, not even looking up to beware of the skis which might poke me, as they bounced along on the shoulders of the skiers hurrying to get something hot to drink. . . .

I heard my name. "Madame Schaeffer, *avez-vous trouvé quelque chose?*"

I looked up to see Monsieur G., a real estate dealer, to whom we had talked several days before. He had not shown us one chalet even, as he said everything he had was "de luxe" and far above the price range we had mentioned. I was surprised that he had even remembered my name. I answered, "*Non, Monsieur G. . . . rien.*"

His reply to that was to step over to his car, open the door and say, "Hop in, I think I have something that might interest you." . . .

We drove on down the mountainside for a few minutes . . . fog blotting out the view, and weariness blotting out any enthusiasm on my part. The car came to stop right beside a Postal Bus stop sign, and a mailbox. We climbed out and went up a pair of log steps, buried in the snow, and opening a gate made our way through unbroken snow to a door opening from a step, level with the ground at the front of the chalet. . . . We went over the chalet together: three floors, made into three apartments; small kitchens, no living room for teas and discussions—but a big place, really, and suitable. There I was, within the half-hour, not because I had had wisdom or cleverness to find it, but because God had answered my prayer. This I believed to be the only explanation.

I arranged with Mr. G. to meet him the next morning with my husband. As I watched him turn the car to start back up to Villars, something occurred to me.

"Oh Mr. G., I forgot to ask . . . how much is the rent?"

"Oh it's not for rent," he replied, "it's for sale" . . . and then the car shot forward on up the road.

"For sale," I repeated to myself dully. "For sale! We have no money, and even if we were millionaires, who would buy a house in a country without having a permit to live there?"

This seemed the last straw to me for a few moments. I was feeling sick with exhaustion by this time anyway, both from sleeplessness and the emotional struggle. Then as I rode down on the bus, and up on the train, I began to review the last days, and the last hours of that particular day. It seemed to me that the "markers" or "signposts" of answered prayer indicated very definitely that God had been leading up to *this* point. Surely He would not lead to a dead end, and the next step on this path was to return and look at this place the next day. Before I arrived back at Chalet Bijou, I was convinced that God had given me a clear sign and that I must go back the next day to that chalet to which *He* had taken me that afternoon.

When I arrived home, it was to discuss the most recent news they had received. "Berne has given us an extension of time. That is we may stay in Switzerland until the matter has been studied, but Sion has sent word they will give *no* extension of time and we have to be out of this chalet and this village and this canton by midnight March 31st. . . .

Also that evening, a phone call came from the lawyer in Lausanne who was collecting the fine letters villagers were writing on our behalf, and the petition, and so on, to say, "You must hurry to find a house, as those papers must be filed within a day or two now."

Both these pieces of news underlined my certainty that the next step was to go back to look at Chalet les Mélèzes in Huémoz. . . .

That night I prayed again, fervently communicating my fears and uncertainties as to my own honesty in wanting God's will, as well as concerning the situation. . . . It was after a length of time during which I had been inwardly struggling for reality in my sincerity of wanting God's will, when I came to this specific request concerning the chalet. It was then that suddenly I became flooded with a surge of assurance that God can do anything, nothing is impossible to Him. My sentence changed in the middle, and

I ended my prayer with a definite plea, which even startled me as I asked it, "Oh, please show us Thy will about this house tomorrow, and if we are to buy it, send us a sign that will be clear enough to convince Fran as well as me, send us one thousand dollars before ten o'clock tomorrow morning."

The following morning as we went through new layers of fresh snow to the train, the postman—his packages and mailbag on a sled—handed us three letters. We opened these on the train, as the morning sun suddenly slipped over the rim of the mountains and poured light and warmth over the light wooden seats. One was from Paris, the next from Belgium . . . and the third was from a man and his wife in the United States. Mr. and Mrs. Salisbury had been following our work with interest and prayer for quite some time, ever since they had been spiritually helped through Fran's messages in a conference they had attended. However, they had never given financial help to our work in any way, nor were they wealthy. They knew that we had been told to leave Switzerland and had been following the story up to that point. It was Mrs. Salisbury who wrote the letter:

"I have a story to tell you that will interest you," she began. "Three months ago Art came home from work with an unexpected amount of money. We decided at first to buy a new car, then came to the conclusion that we didn't need a new car. Our next thought was to invest in buying a little house, which we would rent. We went to look at houses, and as we looked over a very likely small house I saw signs of termites in the beams. 'Look, Art,' I said, 'Doesn't that remind you of the verse in Matthew which says, "Lay not up for yourselves treasures upon earth, where moth and rust doth corrupt, . . . but lay up for yourselves treasure in Heaven, where neither moth nor rust doth corrupt.'" I then asked, 'Art, would you be willing to take this money and invest it literally in Heaven?' . . . He replied, 'Yes, Helen, I would.'

"Well . . . that was three months ago, and all during these three months we have been asking God to show us what He would have us do with this money. Now tonight we have come to a definite decision, and both of us feel certain that we are meant to send you this money . . . to buy a house somewhere that will always be open to young people."

The amount of money was exactly one thousand dollars!

Chapter Four

COMFORT OF FAITH

And I will pray the Father, and he shall give you another Comforter, that he may abide with you for ever; But the Comforter, which is the Holy Ghost, whom the Father will send in my name, he shall teach you all things, and bring all things to your remembrance, whatsoever I have said unto you.

—JOHN 14:16, 26

The sun breaks through the Douglas fir trees near North Bend, Oregon.

I Heard the Voice of Jesus Say

I heard the voice of Jesus say,
    "Come unto me and rest;
Lay down, thou weary one, lay down
    Thy head upon my breast."
I came to Jesus as I was,
    Weary and worn and sad;
I found in Him a resting-place,
    And He has made me glad.

I heard the voice of Jesus say,
    "Behold, I freely give
The living water; thirsty one,
    Stoop down and drink and live."
I came to Jesus, and I drank
    Of that life-giving stream;
My thirst was quenched, my soul
      revived,
    And now I live in Him.

I heard the voice of Jesus say,
    "I am this dark world's light;
Look unto me, thy morn shall rise,
    And all thy day be bright."
I looked to Jesus, and I found
    In Him my Star, my Sun;
And in that light of life I'll walk
    Till traveling days are done.

Horatius Bonar

*Be merciful unto me, O God,
be merciful unto me: for my
soul trusteth in thee: yea, in
the shadow of thy wings will
I make my refuge.*
—Psalm 57:1

"Lo, I Am with You Always"

Wide fields of corn along the valleys spread;
The rain and dew mature the swelling vine.
I see the Lord in multiplying bread;
I see Him turning water into wine.
I see Him working all the works divine
He wrought when Salemward His steps were led.
The selfsame miracles around Him shine;

He feeds the famished, He revives the dead.
He pours the flood of light on darkened eyes;
He chases tears, diseases, fiends away.
His throne is raised upon these orient skies;
His footstool is the pave whereon we pray.
Ah, tell me not of Christ in Paradise,
For He is all around us here today.

John Charles Earle

Life's Lessons

I learn, as the years roll onward
   And leave the past behind,
That much I had counted sorrow
   But proves that God is kind;

That many a flower I had longed for
   Had hidden a thorn of pain,
And many a rugged bypath
   Led to fields of ripened grain.

We must stand in the deepest shadow
   To see the clearest light;
And often through wrong's own darkness
   Comes the very strength of light.

The sweetest rest is at even,
   After a wearisome day,
When the heavy burden of labor
   Has borne from our hearts away;

And those who have never known sorrow
   Can not know the infinite peace
That falls on the troubled spirit
   When it sees at last release.

We must live through the dreary winter
   If we would value the spring;
And the woods must be cold and silent
   Before the robins sing.

The flowers must be buried in darkness
   Before they can bud and bloom,
And the sweetest, warmest sunshine
   Comes after the storm and gloom.

AUTHOR UNKNOWN

A field of wildflowers proclaim the natural beauty of spring at Bird Creek Meadows, Washington.

Prayers

of

Comfort

O Lord Jesus Christ, the same yesterday, today, and forever; O Saviour of the ever-loving heart, we have grieved and wounded Thee. By our willfulness, by our moral cowardice, by our thoughtlessness, by our self-seeking we share in crucifying Thee afresh. By the revelation Thou has made of eternal love, help us to enter into the travail of Thy soul; and by loving self-sacrifice, blend our wills with Thy will to bring all men to a knowledge of the Father. Amen.

Author Unknown

Almighty God, our Heavenly Father, who declarest Thy glory and showest forth Thy handiwork in the heavens and in the earth, deliver us, we beseech Thee, in our several callings, from bondage to the service of self; that we may do the work which Thou has given us to do in truth, in beauty, and in righteousness, with singleness of heart as Thy servants, and to the benefit of our fellowmen; for the sake of Him who came among us as one that serveth, Thy Son, Jesus Christ our Lord.

Book of Common Prayer

I know not by what methods rare, but this I know: God answers prayer. I know that He has given His word and tells me that my prayer is always heard and will be answered, soon or late. And so I pray and calmly wait.

I know not if the blessing sought will come in just the way I thought. But leave my prayers with Him alone, whose will is wiser than my own, assured that He will grant my quest, or send some answer far more blest.

Eliza M. Hickok

O God, who hast drawn over weary day the restful veil of night, wrap our consciences in Heavenly peace. Lift from our hands our tasks, and all through the night bear in Thy bosom the full weight of our burdens and sorrows, that in untroubled slumber we may press our weakness close to Thy strength and win new power for the morrow's duty from Thee who givest Thy beloved sleep. Amen.

CHARLES H. BRENT

I will turn their mourning into joy, and will comfort them, and make them rejoice from their sorrow.

—JEREMIAH 31:13B

Keep us this night, O Lord, from all works of darkness; and whether we wake or sleep, let our thoughts and deeds be in accordance with Thy holy will. Preserve us from all dangers and terrors of the night, from restless watching and sorrowful thoughts, from unnecessary or fretful care and imaginary fears. Let us awake tomorrow renewed in strength and cheerful in spirit; may we arise with holy thoughts and go forth to live to Thine honor, to the service of our fellowmen, and the comfort and joy of our households.

CASPER NEUMANN

O Divine Master, grant that I may not so much seek to be consoled as to console, not so much to be understood as to understand, not so much to be loved as to love; for it is in giving that we receive, it is in pardoning that we are pardoned, it is in dying that we awake to eternal life.

SAINT FRANCIS OF ASSISI

O God, who hast made this fair world and given it to all men richly to enjoy, help me never to grow dull to all its wonder. Because so many of its glories are familiar, let me not forget how wonderful they are. Keep my eyes open to the beauty of blue sky, to the changing pageant of the clouds, to the silver mystery of moonlight, and to the majesty of silent stars. May I feel in every sunrise a miracle of life and light renewed and in every sunset a pledge of Thine unfading light without which we cannot face the dark. So may no single day be common but may each one bring the benediction of its immortal brightness to my soul, through Jesus Christ our Lord.

W. RUSSELL BOWIE

Whatever Is, Is Best

I know, as my life grows older
    And mine eyes have clearer sight,
That under each rank wrong somewhere
    There lies the root of right;

That each sorrow has its purpose,
    By the sorrowing oft unguessed;
But as sure as the sun brings morning,
    Whatever is, is best.

I know that each sinful action,
    As sure as the night brings shade,
Is somewhere, sometime punished,
    Tho' the hour be long delayed.

I know that the soul is aided
    Sometimes by the heart's unrest,
And to grow means often to suffer,
    But whatever is, is best.

I know there are no errors
    In the great eternal plan,
And all things work together
    For the final good of man.

And I know when my soul speeds onward
    In its grand eternal quest,
I shall say as I look back earthward,
    Whatever is, is best.

Ella Wheeler Wilcox

*The seagulls seem to be the only witnesses to the clouds that radiate
from the rock at Second Beach Olympic National Park in Washington.*

Upon the Burning of Our House

In silent night when rest I took
For sorrow near I did not look.
I waken'd was with thundering noise
And piteous shrieks of dreadful voice.
That fearful sound of "Fire!" and "Fire!"
Let no man know is my desire.

I, starting up, the light did spy,
And to my God my heart did cry
To strengthen me in my distress,
And not to leave me succourless.
Then coming out, beheld apace
The flame consume my dwelling place.

And when I could no longer look,
I blest His Name that gave and took,
That laid my goods now in the dust.
Yea, so it was, and so 'twas just.
It was His own: it was not mine;
Far be it that I should repine.

He might of all justly bereft,
But yet sufficient for us left.
When by the ruins oft I past,
My sorrowing eyes aside did cast,
And here and there the places spy,
Where oft I sat and long did lie.

Here stood that trunk, and there that chest;
There lay that store I counted best.
My pleasant things in ashes lie,

And them behold no more shall I.
Under thy roof no guest shall sit,
Nor at thy table eat a bit.

No pleasant tale shall e'er be told,
Nor things recounted done of old.
No candle e'er shall shine in thee,
Nor bridegroom's voice e'er heard shall be.
In silence ever shalt thou lie;
Adieu, Adieu; all's vanity.

Then straight I 'gin my heart to chide
And did thy wealth on earth abide?
Didst fix thy hope on moldering dust,
The arm of flesh didst make thy trust?
Raise up thy thoughts above the sky
That dunghill mists away may fly.

Thou has a house on high erect,
Fram'd by that mighty Architect,
With glory richly furnished,
Stands permanent though this be fled.
It's purchased and paid for too
By Him who hath enough to do.

A prize so vast as is unknown,
Yet, by His Gift, is made thine own.
There's wealth enough, I need no more;
Farewell my pelf, farewell my store.
The world no longer let me love,
My hope and treasure lies Above.

Anne Bradstreet

The sun rises over the Snake River near Richland, Oregon.

MY FAITH LOOKS UP TO THEE

Ray Palmer, 1808-1887

Lowell Mason, 1792-1872

1. My faith looks up to Thee, Thou Lamb of
2. May Thy rich grace im - part Strength to my
3. While life's dark maze I tread, And griefs a -
4. When ends life's tran - sient dream, When death's cold,

Cal - va - ry, Sav - ior di - vine!
faint - ing heart, My zeal in - spire;
round me spread, Be Thou my Guide;
sul - len stream Shall o'er me roll;

Now hear me while I pray,
As Thou hast died for me,
Bid dark - ness turn to day,
Blest Sav - iour, then, in love,

GOD MEANS US TO BE HAPPY

God means us to be happy;
He fills the short-lived years
With loving, tender mercies—
With smiles as well as tears.
Flowers blossom by the pathway
Or, withering, they shed
Their sweetest fragrance over
The bosoms of our dead.

God filled the earth with beauty.
He touched the hills with light;
He crowned the waving forest
With living verdure bright.
He taught the bird to carol,
He gave the wind its voice;
And to the smallest insect
Its moment to rejoice.

What life hath not its blessing?
Who hath not songs to sing
Or grateful words to utter
Or wealth of love to bring?
No way is dark and dreary
If God be with us there;
No danger can befall us
When sheltered by His care.

AUTHOR UNKNOWN

CREDO

Not what, but Whom, I do believe
    That in my darkest hour of need
    Hath comfort that no mortal creed
    To mortal man may give.

Not what, but Whom!
    For Christ is more than all the creeds,
    And His full life of gentle deeds
    Shall all the creeds outlive.

Not what I do believe, but Whom!
    Who walks beside me in the gloom?
    Who shares the burden wearisome?
    Who all the dim way doth illume
    And bids me look beyond the tomb
    The larger life to live?

Not what I do believe,
    But Whom!
    Not what,
    But Whom!

JOHN OXENHAM

TO ONE IN SORROW

Let me come in where you are weeping, friend, and let me take
    your hand.
I who have known a sorrow such as yours can understand.
Let me come in. I would be very still beside you in your grief.
I would not bid you cease your weeping, friend; tears bring relief.
Let me come in. I would only breathe a prayer and hold
    your hand;
For I have known a sorrow such as yours and understand.

GRACE NOLL CROWELL

A NEW DAY

My child,
This is the day I have made for you.
Accept it gladly,
Dance into it,
And carry with you
The joy of resurrection,
The peace of self-giving,
The love that forgives and gives.
Delight yourself in this day
As a child delights
In all that is new.
Revel in it,
Absorb it.
For it is today, new,
That day that I have made.
MYRTLE HALL

Blessed be God, even the Father of our
Lord Jesus Christ, the Father of mercies, and the God of all comfort; Who
comforteth us in all our tribulation, that
we may be able to comfort them which
are in any trouble, by the comfort where-
with we ourselves are comforted of God.

—2 CORINTHIANS 1:3–4

*Water cascades down a cliff near
Hana, Maui, Hawaii, while below,
the crepe ginger blooms.*

TO COMFORT ALL THAT MOURN

CATHERINE MARSHALL

M*ost* people accept intellectually a belief in some kind of life after death. But usually it remains a theoretical belief until death invades one's immediate family circle. . . .

At that time, the first need of the bereaved person is for comfort—just plain comfort. In sorrow, we are all like little children, hurt children who yearn to creep into a mother's arms and rest there; have her stroke our foreheads and speak softly to us as she used to do. But, of course, that is impossible; we are grown men and women. Yet the need for comfort remains.

Our God has promised precisely that. "Comfort ye, comfort ye my people, saith your God." "For thus saith the Lord . . . As one whom his mother comforteth, so will I comfort you."

Strangely, in my case I was given the beginning of that experience of comfort a few hours prior to my husband's death. That morning Peter had wakened about three-thirty with severe pains in his arms and chest. The doctor had come as quickly as he could. He had insisted that Dr. Marshall be taken immediately to the hospital.

As we had waited for the ambulance, Peter had looked up at me through his pain and said, "Catherine, don't try to come with me. We mustn't leave Wee Peter alone in this big house. You can come to the hospital in the morning."

Reluctantly, I had agreed. I knew that he was right, though I wanted so much to be with him.

After the ambulance had come and gone, I went back upstairs and sank to my knees beside the bed. There was the need for prayer, for this was an emergency indeed. It could mean only one thing—another massive heart attack. But how was I to pray? Swirling emotions had plunged my mind into utter confusion.

Suddenly, the unexpected happened. Over the turbulent emotions there crept a strange, all-pervading peace. And through and around me flowed love as I had never before experienced it. It was as if body and spirit were floating on a cloud, resting—as if Someone who loved me very much were wrapping me round and round with His love.

I knelt there marveling at what was

The waves roll onto Smelt Sands State Park, Oregon.

happening. I had done nothing, said nothing, to bring it about. Through my mind trooped a quick procession of thoughts . . . *Maybe this is what the Bible means by that lovely statement—"underneath are the everlasting arms." That describes exactly what I'm feeling.*

But what did this mean in relation to Peter, his ailing heart, and the emergency that threatened us? I thought it meant that everything was going to be all right, that Peter would be healed. There seemed to be nothing for which to ask God. Presence was all around me. So my prayer took the form simply of thanking Him for the miracle that His love could be such a personal love; for His tender care of Peter and Wee Peter and me.

At 8:15 that same morning, Peter had stepped across the boundary that divides this life from the next. Then I knew that the experience of the night before had meant something far different. I had been granted it so that when the blow fell, I might have the certainty that a loving Father had not deserted me.

It is of the Lord's mercies that we are not consumed, because his compassions fail not. They are new every morning: great is thy faithfulness. The Lord is my portion, saith my soul; therefore will I hope in him. The Lord is good unto them that wait for him, to the soul that seeketh him. It is good that a man should both hope and quietly wait for the salvation of the Lord.

—LAMENTATIONS 3:22–26

MY LORD AND MY ALL

If ask'd, what of Jesus I think?
Though still my best thoughts are but poor,
I say, He's my meat and my drink,
My life, and my strength, and my store;
My shepherd, my husband, my friend,
My Saviour from sin and from thrall;
My hope from beginning to end,
My portion, my Lord, and my all.

JOHN NEWTON

O HOLY SAVIOUR, FRIEND UNSEEN

O Holy Saviour, friend unseen,
Since on Thine arm Thou bidd'st me lean,
Help me throughout life's changing scene
    By faith to cling to Thee.

What though the world deceitful prove
And earthly friends and hopes remove,
With patient, uncomplaining love
    Still would I cling to Thee.

Though oft I seem to tread alone
Life's dreary waste, with thorns o'ergrown,
Thy voice of love, in gentlest tone,
    Still whispers, "Cling to me!"

Though faith and hope are often tried,
I ask not, need not, aught beside;
So safe, so calm, so satisfied,
    The soul that clings to Thee.

CHARLOTTE ELLIOTT

The sun catches the Three Patriarchs as the north fork of the Virgin River remains in shadow at Zion National Park, Utah.

Chapter Five

JOY OF FAITH

I will greatly rejoice in the Lord, my soul shall be joyful in my God; for he hath clothed me with the garments of salvation, he hath covered me with the robe of righteousness, as a bridegroom decketh himself with ornaments, and as a bride adorneth herself with her jewels.

—ISAIAH 61:10

A summer day dawns over the vineyards near Alpine, Oregon.

ACCEPT OUR TRIBUTE

Jesus, Thou everlasting King,
Accept the tribute which we bring;
Accept Thy well-deserved renown
And wear our praises as Thy crown.

Let every act of worship be
Like our espousals, Lord, to Thee;
Like the blest hour when from above
We first received the pledge of love.

The gladness of that happy day,
Oh may it ever, ever stay.
Nor let our faith forsake its hold,
Nor hope decline, nor love grow cold.

Let every moment, as it flies,
Increase Thy praise, improve our joys,
Till we are raised to sing Thy name,
At the great supper of the Lamb.

ISAAC WATTS

O come, let us sing unto the Lord: let us make a joyful noise to the rock of our salvation. Let us come before his presence with thanksgiving, and make a joyful noise unto him with psalms.

—PSALM 95:1–2

PRAISE TO THE CREATOR

Ye nations of the earth rejoice
Before the Lord, your Sovereign King.
Serve Him with cheerful heart and voice;
With all your tongues His glory sing.

The Lord is God; 'tis He alone
Doth life and breath and being give.
We are His work, and not our own;
The sheep that on His pasture live.

Enter His gates with songs of joy;
With praises to His courts repair;
And make it your divine employ
To pay your thanks and honours there.

The Lord is good; the Lord is kind.
Great is His grace, His mercy sure;
And the whole race of man shall find
His truth from age to age endure.

ISAAC WATTS

A stream from the aptly named Swift
Current Lake tumbles down its channel
while Grinnell Point rises in the distance at
Glacier National Park, Montana.

GOD'S GRANDEUR

The world is charged with the grandeur of God.
It will flame out, like shining from shook foil;
It gathers to a greatness, like the ooze of oil
Crushed. Why do men then now not reck His rod?
Generations have trod, have trod, have trod;
And all is seared with trade; bleared, smeared with toil;
And wears man's smudge and shares man's smell: the soil
Is bare now, nor can foot feel, being shod.

And for all this, nature is never spent;
There lives the dearest freshness deep down things;
And though the last lights off the black West went
Oh, morning, at the brown brink eastward, springs—
Because the Holy Ghost over the bent
World broods with warm breast and with ah! bright wings.
GERARD MANLEY HOPKINS

I HEARD HIM

I heard the great Creator's voice speak softly in the breeze.
I heard Him when He rustled all the branches in the trees.
I heard Him in the patter of a cool, refreshing shower,
And in the mighty river's boom I heard Him speak with power.
I heard Him in the chatter of a squirrel all dressed in fur,
And in the sweet contentment of a fuzzy kitten's purr.
I heard Him in the cricket's chirp one starry, summer night,
And when the saucy rooster crowed announcing morning's light.
I heard Him in a waterfall and in a singing creek,
And in the whisper of the pines, I'm sure I heard Him speak.
I felt the great Creator near in all His wondrous ways
And then I paused to bow my head in gratitude and praise.
ELEANOR LYONS CULVER

*Brilliant colors adorn the trees along
the Metolius River in Oregon.*

PRAYERS

OF JOY

We give Thee thanks, O God, for great moments of joy and strength that come to us when, by a strong and special movement of grace, we are able to perform some act of pure and disinterested love. For the clean fire of that love which floods the soul and cleanses the whole man and leaves us filled with an unexpected lightness and freedom for action. For the moment of pure prayer which not only establishes order in the soul, but even fortifies us against physical weariness and brings us a new lease on life itself. Glory be to Thee for Thy precious gift!

THOMAS MERTON

Ask, and ye shall receive, that your joy may be full.

—JOHN 16:24B

Rejoicing and eternal praise be to you, my Lord Jesus Christ, who sent the Holy Spirit into the hearts of your disciples and increased the boundless love of God in their spirits. Blessed are you, praiseworthy and glorious forever, my Lord Jesus.

SAINT BIRGITTA

Almighty God, grant that I may awake to the joy of this day, finding gladness in all its toil and difficulty and in its pleasure and success, in all its failures and sorrow; teach me to throw open the windows of my life, that I may look always away from myself and behold the need of the world. Give me the will and strength to bring the gift of Thy gladness to others of Thy children, that with them I may stand to bear the burden and heat of the day and offer Thee the praise of work well done, through Jesus Christ our Lord. Amen.

AUTHOR UNKNOWN

My God, I thank Thee who hast made the earth so bright, so full of splendor and of joy, beauty, and light; so many glorious things are here, noble and right. I thank Thee too that Thou hast made joy to abound; so many gentle thoughts and deeds circling us round; that in the darkest spot of earth some love is found.

I thank Thee more that all our joy is touched with pain; that shadows fall on brightest hours; that thorns remain, so that earth's bliss may be our guide and not our chain. For Thou, who knowest, Lord, how soon our weak heart clings, hast given us joys, tender and true, yet all with wings; so that we see, gleaming on high, diviner things.

ADELAIDE A. PROCTOR

My God, I pray that I may so know You and love You that I may rejoice in You. And if I may not do so fully in this life let me go steadily on to the day when I come to that fullness. . . .

Let me receive that which You promised through Your truth, that my joy may be full.

SAINT ANSELM

O Lord Christ, help us to maintain ourselves in simplicity and in joy—the joy of the merciful, the joy of brotherly love. Grant that, renouncing henceforth all thought of looking back, and joyful with infinite gratitude, we may never fear to precede the dawn, to praise and bless and sing to the Christ our Lord.

TAIZE COMMUNITY

Almighty and Holy Spirit—the Comforter, pure, living, true— illuminate, govern, sanctify me, and confirm my heart and mind in the faith, and in all genuine consolation; preserve and rule over me that, dwelling in the house of the Lord all the days of my life, to behold the beauty of the Lord, I may be and remain forever in the temple of the Lord, and praise Him with a joyful spirit and in union with all the Heavenly Church.

PHILIPP MELANCHTHON

Sing, O heavens; and be joyful, O earth; and break forth into singing, O mountains: for the Lord hath comforted his people, and will have mercy upon his afflicted.

—Isaiah 49:13

GOD GIVE ME JOY

God give me joy in the common things:
In the dawn that lures, the eve that sings,

In the new grass sparkling after rain,
In the late wind's wild and weird refrain,

In the springtime's spacious field of gold,
In the precious light by winter doled.

God give me joy in the love of friends,
In their dear home talk as summer ends,

In the songs of children, unrestrained,
In the sober wisdom age has gained.

God give me joy in the tasks that press,
In the memories that burn and bless,

In the thought that life has love to spend,
In the faith that God's at journey's end.

God give me hope for each day that springs.
God give me joy in the common things.

THOMAS CURTIS CLARK

ALL PEOPLE THAT ON EARTH DO DWELL

All people that on earth do dwell,
Sing to the Lord with cheerful voice.
Him serve with mirth, His praise forth tell;
Come ye before Him and rejoice.

The Lord, ye know, is God indeed;
Without our aid He did us make.
We are His folk, He doth us feed,
And for His sheep He doth us take.

Oh, enter then His gates with praise;
Approach with joy His courts unto.
Praise, laud, and bless His Name always,
For it is seemly so to do.

For why? The Lord our God is good;
His mercy is forever sure.
His truth at all times firmly stood
And shall from age to age endure.

To Father, Son, and Holy Ghost,
The God Whom Heaven and earth adore,
From men and from the angel host
Be praise and glory evermore.

WILLIAM KETHE

The sky itself rejoices at the break of dawn over the Willamette Valley of Oregon.

Make a joyful noise unto the Lord, all the earth:
make a loud noise, and rejoice, and sing praise. Sing
unto the Lord with the harp; with the harp, and the
voice of a psalm. With trumpets and sound of cornet
make a joyful noise before the Lord, the King.
—PSALM 98:4–6

GOD'S WORLD

I'm glad I am living this morning
    Because the day is so fair,
And I feel God's presence so keenly
    About me everywhere.

The heavens declare His glory.
    The trees seem to speak of His power;
And I see His matchless beauty
    In each small, growing flower.

The rocks all tell of His wonder.
    In the hills His strength I see;
And the birds are singing His praises
    In the songs that they sing to me.

Oh, I'm glad to be living this morning
    In a world of beauty so rare
Where the God of Heaven is hovering
    About me everywhere.

MILDRED KEELING

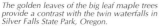

The golden leaves of the big leaf maple trees
provide a contrast with the twin waterfalls in
Silver Falls State Park, Oregon.

Joyful, Joyful We Adore Thee

Henry Van Dyke, 1852-1933

Ludwig van Beethoven, 1770-1827
Adapted by Edward Hodges

1. Joy - ful, joy - ful, we a - dore Thee,
2. All Thy works with joy sur - round Thee,
3. Mor - tals, join the might - y cho - rus,

God of glo - ry, Lord of love; Hearts un - fold like
Earth and heav'n re - flect Thy rays, Stars and an - gels
Which the morn - ing stars be - gan; Fa - ther - love is

flow'rs be - fore Thee, Prais - ing Thee, their sun a - bove.
sing a - round Thee, Cen - ter of un - bro - ken praise:
reign - ing o'er us, Broth - er - love binds man to man.

A merry heart doeth good like a medicine.

—PROVERBS 17:22

YE HEAVENS, UPLIFT YOUR VOICE

Ye heav'ns, uplift your voice;
Sun, moon, and stars rejoice
And thou too nether earth,
Join in the common mirth.

For winter storm at last
And rain is over-past;
Instead whereof the green
And fruitful palm is seen.

Ye flow'rs of spring appear,
Your gentle heads uprear
And let the growing seed
Enamel lawn and mead.

Ye birds with open throat
Prolong your sweetest note;
Awake, ye blissful choirs,
And strike your merry lyres.

For why? Unhurt by death,
The Lord of Life and Breath,
Jesus, as He foresaid,
Is risen from the dead.

FIFTEENTH-CENTURY CAROL

The shade and green moss surrounding Soda Creek Falls offer a cooling respite on a summer day in Cascadia State Park, Oregon.

THE JOY OF FRIENDSHIP

PAMELA KENNEDY

I was browsing in a gift shop the other day and a small wall hanging caught my eye. On a piece of rough board the artist had painted a colorful garden. Small, lavender violets clustered in front of a row of daisies. Behind these, roses and snapdragons bloomed. A line of sunflowers stood guard at the garden's border, and in the distance a sheltering barrier of evergreens filled the background. Arched over the top of the plaque were the words "Friendship Is Life's Garden."

This idea of friendship as a garden intrigued me. I mentally inventoried my friends, deciding who was a sensitive violet, who a cheerful daisy, which ones were elegant roses, and which were practical and optimistic sunflowers. I must admit I even ventured to identify a few weeds in my musings! Then I recalled the row of trees standing in the background of the artist's scene. I'm not sure if these were meant to be included in friendship's garden, but for me they became a powerful image of a very special kind of friend I treasure—my long-distance friends.

Thirty years of marriage to a military man have offered many wonderful opportunities to make new friends and an equal number of occasions to leave them behind as we moved thousands of miles away to a new assignment. Some of my more stationary acquaintances doubt the possibility of maintaining friendships with people one doesn't see for years. I like to tell them distance isn't really a barrier to friendship, it only adds a new dimension to it.

Like the trees in the artist's picture, my long-distance friends offer a sense of perspective to my life. I can see them in memories that tower above the circumstances of today, reminding me of times we shared joy, challenge, sadness, and triumph together. Just like the wind and rain and sun shape the development of a tree, my friends helped to shape me by their influence, example, and encouragement.

I met Nan when she was a patient in a hospital where I was doing volunteer work about twenty-five years ago. I felt so sorry for this beautiful mother of six because she suffered from constant pain and was confined to a wheelchair. With the thought of cheering her up, I visited her often, and we spent several hours sharing our thoughts on life and faith. I'm not sure if my immature attempts to offer solace

A pasture of grass awaits harvesting at Fern Ridge Reservoir in Oregon.

accomplished much in her life, but her wit and wisdom made a profound difference in mine. She gently demonstrated that true joy and peace are more a matter of internal circumstance than external, that a deep and abiding confidence in God transcends our present doubts, and that family is the context in which we learn about love—both giving and receiving.

Her words strengthened me like the nourishing rain strengthens the trunk of a tree, enabling it to grow until it is able to withstand a storm without being broken. I have seen Nan only a handful of times since we were first friends, but each time I feel tested by the winds of a storm, I recall her strength and am encouraged to endure with her grace.

Restore unto me the joy of thy salvation; and uphold me with thy free spirit.

—PSALM 51:12

For his anger endureth but a moment; in his favour is life: weeping may endure for a night, but joy cometh in the morning.

—PSALM 30:5

THE BEST IS YET TO BE

CORRIE TEN BOOM

A person who influenced my life in my late teens was a man from India. As a boy he was taught to hate Jesus. He knew about God, but the Bible of the Christians was a book which he believed was a gigantic lie. Once he took a Bible and burned it, feeling that with this act, he could publicly declare his scorn of what he believed were the untruths it contained. When missionaries passed him, he threw mud on them.

But there was a terrible unrest inside of him; he longed to know God. He told this story about himself:

"Although I had believed that I had done a very good deed by burning the Bible, I felt unhappy. After three days, I couldn't bear it any longer. I rose early in the morning and prayed that if God really existed, He would reveal Himself to me. I wanted to know if there was an existence after death, if there was a Heaven. The only way I could know it for sure was to die. So I decided to die.

"I planned to throw myself in front of the train which passed by our house. Then suddenly something unusual happened. The room was filled with a beautiful glow and I saw a man. I thought it might be Buddha or some other holy man. Then I heard a voice.

" 'How long will you deny Me? I died for you; I have given my life for you.'

"Then I saw His hands—the pierced hands of Jesus Christ. This was the Christ I had imagined as a great man who once lived in Palestine, but who died and disappeared. And yet He now stood before me, alive! I saw His face looking at me with love.

The sun sets over Homoa Beach in Maui, Hawaii.

"Three days before, I had burned the Bible, and yet He was not angry. I was suddenly changed . . . I saw Him as Christ, the living One, the Saviour of the world. I fell on my knees and knew a wonderful peace, which I had never found anywhere before. That was the happiness I had been seeking for such a long time."

When I first heard about Sadhu Singh, the stories seemed to grow, until it was impossible to separate fact from fiction. Then he came to Holland and was asked to come to a weekend conference at Lunteren. I was so excited about the possibility of hearing him that I went to the conference grounds, although I knew it was booked to capacity. . . .

That weekend, as I listened to the Sadhu, I was amazed but disturbed. He told of the visions he had seen—of how he really saw Jesus—at a time when he didn't believe. We had all read about the Apostle Paul's experiences on the road to Damascus, but here was a man who claimed to have had this experience himself. . . .

After the meeting I needed to think,

and so I started to walk through the heather by myself, trying to understand all I had heard, questioning my own relationship with God.

As I was walking, I was deep in my own thoughts and almost ran into the Sadhu, who was going for a stroll too. I worked up my courage to ask him some questions but soon found he was very easy to talk to. He put me completely at ease.

"Please, Mr. Sadhu, tell me what is wrong with me? I'm a child of God, I have received Jesus as my Saviour and I know that my sins are forgiven. I know He is with me for He has said, 'I am with you always till the end of the world.' But what's wrong with me? I've never seen a vision or experienced a miracle."

The Sadhu smiled at me. "Sometimes people come to me to see a miracle. When they come now I'll send them to Corrie ten Boom. That I know Jesus is alive and with me is no miracle . . . these eyes have seen Him. But you, who have never seen Him, know His presence. Isn't that a miracle of the Holy Spirit? Look in your Bible at what Jesus said to Thomas in John 20:29: 'Blessed are they who did not see, and yet believed.' Don't pray for visions; He gives you the assurance of His presence without visions."

It was such a relief to me. . . . it seemed as if the Lord had thrown a curtain aside and I could see the light. Yes, it's a tremendous thing that we can know the Lord is with us! Paul has said "I know in whom I have believed." And Peter . . . how beautifully he expressed it:

"And though you have never seen Him, yet I know that you love Him. At present you trust Him without being able to see Him, and even now He brings you a joy that words cannot express and which has in it a hint of the glories of Heaven; and all the time you are receiving the result of your faith in Him—the salvation of your own souls" (1 Peter 1:8, 9 Phillips).

When I went home after that conference, I couldn't wait to tell what I had experienced. I couldn't stop talking. . . . I tried to recall everything I had heard and finally, when I paused long enough for anyone to comment, Tante Anna said, "It's just as if you have seen and heard one of the disciples of Jesus."

Father said, "Isn't it wonderful to have such joy here on earth? It's a little foretaste of Heaven. Yes, the best is yet to be."

Father often said that after we had shared some particularly rich occurrence.

Years later when Father entered a door of a prison, he said, "Remember, Corrie, the best is yet to be." After ten days, Father's spirit stepped out of that prison and into paradise.

The best had arrived.

The richness of red Indian Paintbrush provides a beautiful contrast to the snow of Mount Ranier, Washington.

Chapter Six

LOVE FROM FAITH

*And now abideth faith, hope,
charity, these three; but the
greatest of these is charity.*

—1 CORINTHIANS 13:13

*An immovable rock stands before an audience of
purple lupines on the coast of Cape Blanco, Oregon.*

Love Passes through All

Thomas à Kempis

Nothing is sweeter than Love, nothing more courageous, nothing higher, nothing wider, nothing more pleasant, nothing fuller nor better in Heaven and earth. Love feels no burden, thinks nothing of trouble, attempts what is above its strength, pleads no excuse of impossibility; for it thinks all things lawful for itself and all things possible. It is therefore able to undertake all things, and it completes many things, and brings them to a conclusion, where he who does not love faints and lies down. Love watcheth, and sleeping, slumbereth not. Though weary, love is not tired; though pressed, it is not straightened; though alarmed, it is not confounded: but as a lively flame, and burning torch, it forces its way upwards, and securely passes through all.

Therefore Give Us Love

Love is kind and suffers long;
Love is meek and thinks no wrong;
Love than death itself more strong;
   Therefore give us love.

Faith will vanish into sight;
Hope be emptied in delight;
Love in Heaven will shine more bright;
   Therefore give us love.

Christopher Wordsworth

Charity suffereth long, and is kind; charity envieth not; charity vaunteth not itself, is not puffed up, Doth not behave itself unseemly, seeketh not her own, is not easily provoked, thinketh no evil; Rejoiceth not in iniquity, but rejoiceth in the truth; Beareth all things, believeth all things, hopeth all things, endureth all things.

—1 Corinthians 13:4–7

Lupines and balsamroot fill the vista with joy on a summer afternoon in Tom McCall Preserve in the Columbia River National Scenic Area, Oregon.

Love from Faith

121

Increasing Love

Leo Tolstoy

I believe in this: I believe in God, whom I understand as Spirit, as Love, as the Source of all. I believe that He is in me and I in Him . . . I believe that man's true welfare lies in fulfilling God's will, and His will is that men should love one another and should consequently do to others as they wish others to do to them—of which it is said in the Gospels that in this is the law and the prophets.

I believe therefore that the meaning of the life of every man is to be found only in increasing the love that is in him; that this increase of love leads man, even in this life, to ever greater and greater blessedness. And after death gives him the more blessedness, and the more love he has, and helps more than anything else toward the establishment of the Kingdom of God on earth; that is, to the establishment of an order of life in which the discord, deception, and violence that now rule will be replaced by free accord, by truth, and by the brotherly love of one for another.

I believe that to obtain progress in love there is only one means: prayer . . . private prayer, like the sample given us by Jesus, consisting of the renewing and strengthening in our consciousness of the meaning of our life and of our complete dependence on the will of God.

And the Lord make you to increase and abound in love one toward another, and toward all men, even as we do toward you.

—1 Thessalonians 3:12

Rolling wheat fields near Colfax, Washington, are ready for the harvest.

Love Bade Me Welcome

Love bade me welcome;
   yet my soul drew back,
Guilty of dust and sin.
But quick-eyed Love,
   observing me grow slack,
Drew nearer to me,
   sweetly questioning,
If I lacked anything.

"A guest," I answered,
   "worthy to be here."
Love said, "You shall be he."
"I, the unkind, ungrateful?
   Ah, my dear,
I cannot look on Thee."

Love took my hand and,
   smiling, did reply,
"Who made the eyes but I?"

"Truth Lord, but I have marred them;
   let my shame
Go where it doth deserve."
"And know you not," says Love,
   "who bore the blame?"
"My dear, then I will serve."
"You must sit down," says Love,
   "and taste my meat."
So I did sit and eat.

GEORGE HERBERT

PRAYERS OF LOVE

Lord God, thank You for loving us even when we turn away from You. We are grateful for Your constant care and concern. Though we feel unworthy of Your great love, we thank You that through our weaknesses You give us strength; and in our wanderings You show us the way.

AUTHOR UNKNOWN

With charity fill Thou my heart, as summer fills the grass with dews; and as the year itself renews in the sun when winter days depart, Blessed Forever, grant Thou me to be renewed in Thee. Amen.

ALICE CAREY

I say unto you, Love your enemies, bless them that curse you, do good to them that hate you, and pray for them which despitefully use you, and persecute you.

—MATTHEW 5:44

Father, grant unto us true family love that we may belong more entirely to those whom Thou hast given us, understanding each other, day by day, more instinctively; forbearing each other, day by day, more patiently; growing, day by day, more closely into oneness with each other.

Father, Thou too art love. Thou knowest the depth of pain and the height of glory which abide continually in love. Make us perfect in love for these our dear ones, as knowing that without them we can never be made perfect in Thee.

Father, bring to full fruit in us Thine own nature, that nature of humble redemptive devotion, which out of two responsive souls, can create a new Heaven and a new earth, one eternal glory of divine self-sharing.

AUTHOR UNKNOWN

Lord of the loving heart, may mine be loving too. Lord of the gentle hands, may mine be gentle too. Lord of the willing feet, may mine be willing too. So may I grow more like Thee in all I say and do.

Author Unknown

Kindle, O Lord, in our hearts, we pray, the flame of that love which never ceases, that it may burn in us and give light to others. May we shine forever in Your temple, set on fire with that eternal light of Yours which puts to flight the darkness of this world; in the name of Jesus Christ, Your Son, our Lord. Amen.

Author Unknown

We love You, O God; and we desire to love You more and more. Grant us that we may love You as much as we desire and as much as we ought. O dearest Friend, who has so loved and saved us, the thought of whom is so sweet and always growing sweeter, come with Christ and dwell in our hearts; then You will keep a watch over our lips, our steps, our deeds, and we shall not need to be anxious either for our souls or our bodies. Give us love, sweetest of all gifts, which knows no enemy. Give us in our hearts pure love, born of Your love to us, that we may love others as You love us.

O most loving Father of Jesus Christ, from whom flows all love, let our hearts, frozen in sin, cold to You and cold to others, be warmed by this divine fire. So help and bless us in Your Son. Amen.

Saint Anselm

Lord God, the God of all goodness and grace, You are worthy of a greater love than we can give or understand: fill our hearts with such love towards You which overcomes laziness and fear, that nothing may seem too hard for us to do or to suffer as we obey You; and grant that in loving You we may become daily more like You, and may finally obtain the crown of life which You have promised to those who love You, through Jesus Christ our Lord. Amen.

Author Unknown

Dear Lord! Kind Lord! Gracious Lord! I pray Thou wilt look on all I love tenderly today. Weed their hearts of weariness; scatter every care down a wake of angel-wings winnowing the air. And with all the needy, oh divide, I pray, this vast treasure of content that is mine today.

James Whitcomb Riley

TODAY

AUTHOR UNKNOWN

Mend a quarrel. Search out a forgotten friend. Dismiss suspicion and replace it with trust. Write a love letter. Share some treasure. Give a soft answer. Encourage youth. Manifest your loyalty in a word or deed.

Keep a promise. Find the tie. Forego a grudge. Forgive an enemy. Listen. Apologize if you were wrong. Try to understand. Flout envy. Examine your demands on others. Think first of someone else. Appreciate, be kind, be gentle. Laugh a little more.

Deserve confidence. Take up arms against malice. Decry complacency. Express your gratitude. Worship your God. Gladden the heart of a child. Take pleasure in the beauty and wonder of the earth.

Speak your love. Speak it again. Speak it still again. Speak it still once again.

LOVE'S PREROGATIVE

Love ever gives, forgives, outlives.
And ever stands with open hands.
And while it lives, it gives.
For this is love's prerogative,
To give and give and give.

JOHN OXENHAM

Many waters cannot quench love, neither can the floods drown it: if a man would give all the substance of his house for love, it would utterly be contemned.

—SONG OF SOLOMON 8:7

Spring arrives along the McKenzie River in Oregon and brings the bright green of tender leaves and moss.

IMMORTAL LOVE, FOREVER FULL

Immortal Love, forever full,
  Forever flowing free,
Forever shared, forever whole,
  A never ebbing sea!

Our outward lips confess the name
  All other names above;
But love alone knows whence it came
  And comprehendeth love.

Blow, winds of God, awake and blow
  The mists of earth away!
Shine out, O Light divine, and show
  How wide and far we stray!

The letter fails, the systems fall,
  And every symbol wanes;
The Spirit overbrooding all,
  Eternal Love remains.
Amen.

JOHN GREENLEAF WHITTIER

THE CALL

Come, my Way, my Truth, my Life:
Such a Way as gives us breath,
Such a Truth as ends all strife,
Such a Life as killeth death.

Come, my Light, my Feast, my
    Strength:
Such a Light as shows a feast,
Such a Feast as mends in length,
Such a Strength as makes his guest.

Come, my Joy, my Love, my Heart:
Such a Joy as none can move,
Such a Love as none can part,
Such a Heart as joys in love.

GEORGE HERBERT

The Lord hath appeared of old unto me, saying,
Yea, I have loved thee with an everlasting love:
therefore with lovingkindness have I drawn thee.

—JEREMIAH 31:3

*The splendor of the
south falls is surrounded
by big leaf maple trees
in Silver Falls State
Park, Oregon.*

LOVE LIFTED ME

James Rowe, 1865-1933

Howard E. Smith, 1863-1918

1. I was sink - ing deep in sin, Far from the peace - ful shore,
2. All my heart to Him I give, Ev - er to Him I'll cling,
3. Souls in dan - ger, look a - bove, Je - sus com - plete - ly saves;

Ver - y deep - ly stained with - in, Sink - ing to rise no more;
In His bless - ed pres - ence live, Ev - er His prais - es sing.
He will lift you by His love Out of the an - gry waves.

But the Mas - ter of the sea Heard my de - spair - ing cry,
Love so might - y and so true Mer - its my soul's best songs;
He's the Mas - ter of the sea, Bil - lows His will o - bey;

From the wa-ters lift - ed me, Now safe am I.
Faith - ful, lov - ing serv - ice, too, To Him be - longs.
He your Sav - ior wants to be— Be saved to - day.

Love lift - ed me! Love lift - ed me!
e - ven me! e - ven me!

When noth - ing else could help, Love lift-ed me. Love lift-ed me.

FOUNDATIONS OF FAITH

WAYNE SIMSIC

The whole of the Scriptures provides us with the foundation of faith: God loves us and has maintained this love faithfully through all generations. . . . Our God is a real God in whom we can have faith.

Christians believe that the covenant is most powerfully expressed in Jesus Christ. God's heart is so set on us that God sent Jesus the Christ to save us. Jesus' entire life—birth, death, and resurrection—was an expression of the unconditional, eternal love of God, and it initiated a new phase in God's relation with us. At the heart of the Christian belief is faith in the person of Jesus Christ.

Jesus is the incarnated testament to God's faithfulness.

WHO WILL LEAD ME INTO EDOM?

PSALM 60:9

Who will lead me into Edom?
   Who will take me by the hand?
Who will break the rugged pathway
   Leading through that unknown land?

Hope will lead me into Edom;
   Hope will guide me all the way.
Like the morning star before me,
   Hope will bring me to the day.

Faith will lead me into Edom—
   Faith, eternal as the hills,
Faith which passeth understanding
   And all prophecy fulfills.

Love will lead me into Edom
   Like a father leads a child—
Love as gentle as the breezes,
   As benign and undefiled.

Christ will lead me into Edom;
   Christ will guide and guard and keep,
Like a shepherd on the hillside
   Loves and leads his trusting sheep.

God will guide me into Edom
   And my splendid destiny—
God fulfilling every promise
   Of my immortality.

WILLIAM L. STIDGER

*The trail disappears into the rolling hills
at the foot of Steen's Mountain, Oregon.*

LOVE FROM FAITH

The King of Love My Shepherd Is

The King of love my Shepherd is,
  Whose goodness faileth never;
I nothing lack if I am His,
  And He is mine forever.

Where streams of living water flow,
  My ransomed soul He leadeth,
And where the verdant pastures grow
  With food celestial feedeth.

Perverse and foolish oft I strayed,
  But yet in love He sought me;
And on His shoulder gently laid,
  And home, rejoicing, brought me.

In death's dark vale I fear no ill
  With Thee, dear Lord, beside me;
Thy rod and staff my comfort still,
  Thy cross before to guide me.

And so through all the length of days,
  Thy goodness faileth never.
Good Shepherd, may I sing Thy praise
  Within Thy house forever.

Henry W. Baker

The Bridge Builder

An old man going a lone highway
Came at the evening, cold and gray,
To a chasm vast and wide and steep
With waters rolling cold and deep.

The old man crossed in the twilight dim.
The sullen stream had no fears for him;
But he turned when safe on the other side,
And built a bridge to span the tide.

"Old man," said a fellow pilgrim near,
"You are wasting your strength with building here.
Your journey will end with the ending day;
You never again will pass this way.
You've crossed the chasm, deep and wide,
Why build you this bridge at eventide?"

The builder lifted his old, gray head.
"Good friend, in the path I have come," he said,
"There followeth after me today
A youth whose feet must pass this way.
The chasm that was as nought to me
To that fair-haired youth may a pitfall be;
He too must cross in the twilight dim.
Good friend, I am building this bridge for him."

Will Allen Dromgoole

And the peace of God, which passeth all understanding,
shall keep your hearts and minds through Christ Jesus.
—Philippians 4:7

The way is narrow through the Oneonta Gorge in Oregon.

THE ULTRA-SUEDE LADIES

I had tea with the Queen," the beautiful lady informed me. "Queen who?" I wanted to ask facetiously. But I knew "who"—Queen Elizabeth, of course—my queen! This beautiful, polished American lady who was to share the platform with me at a women's retreat was telling me all about her tea party with the Queen of England herself! After describing the event in detail, she added another story of yet one more "Queenly" interview in another European capital, where she had been able actually to talk to "Her Majesty" about the Lord! . . .

Looking at my beautiful, ultra-suede companion, I felt the old familiar struggle all over again. I wanted to be like her!

Ultra-suede ladies frightened me out of my mind. I don't mean just the ultra-suede ladies, but the ultra, ultra ones. They threatened me and I had already decided there was absolutely no way that God could use me to reach "the up and outers." I mean "just look at me," I mumbled miserably as I slumped against the upholstery in a self-conscious heap. Here

I was in my forties, suffering the bad self-image teenage syndrome. I wanted to shout at my Maker, "Why don't you recall all those 1935 models with defects [like me] and make us right. For a start, you could give me new hair." It had never "grown up and become adult." It was the fine, baby type that convinced me I faced premature baldness. . . .

Not only would I have liked to have asked the Eternal why He had not given me strong wavy, stay-in-place hair, but I also mulled over the question of why He hadn't made my metabolism so that I could eat all those sweet, sticky, energy-giving cakes and hot fudge sundaes that I wanted and still stay slim and trim. . . . Glancing sideways in the semi-dark cab, I acknowledged the super-trim shape of my companion with something akin to gloom and despair. How would one ever gain the ear of the ultra, ultra-suede ladies unless you looked like a size-eight model? . . .

Then one day I went to Memphis, Tennessee. Verla met me at the airport. She was a speaker and teacher, ran a Rescue Mission, talked to up-and-outers

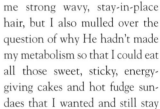

THE IDEALS TREASURY OF FAITH AND INSPIRATION

136

Majestic, snow-covered mountains rim Moraine Lake in Banff National Park, Canada.

and down-and-outers, and was totally relaxed with both. She gave me an outsize uncomfortable feeling in the pit of my conscience the moment I saw her warm touch with the women. We completed our meetings and she was very appreciative of my part, but everything she felt about me came right through her transparent personality. Or maybe she didn't feel like that at all, and it was just that her whole approach and ministry served to rebuke me outright, saying louder than any verbal complaint—"Jill, you are technically a good speaker—BUT you do not love these women!" Being with her was like telling me my slip was showing—it was a

different sort of slip this time—it was the slip of disobedience that was hanging down several inches. I knew that love was a conscious decision. Also I knew, where these women were concerned, I had definitely decided against love.

The Eternal had long since shown me that love was not just a feeling too big for words, for Jesus had said to His followers, "A new commandment I give unto you, that ye love one another." I knew that you couldn't command a feeling, and so had come to the conclusion that if love was a command, then I must be able to obey it; which took it out of the realm of emotions and into the area of actions . . . loving

An outcropping of the rock of a sand dune reminds us of possible dangers to boats at Cape Kiwanda, Oregon.

actions that would involve me in the lives of people I didn't "feel" I even liked. . . .

In the days that followed, I asked myself if it was simply my Britishness that forbade the crossing of the "class" line or was my problem just inverted pride? Perhaps it was false humility or a despising of the gifts that others saw in me. I didn't know what was so dreadfully wrong and so I continued to travel and speak and wonder afterward how on earth I'd had the nerve!

And then one day the Eternal decided it was time to set me free. I was in Coral Gables, Florida, among some of the *nou-*

veau riche young ladies who populate that classy area of Miami. . . . Observing them as they entered the club restaurant where we were dining, each one seemed a beauty in her own lovely right. Sitting at a table with three of the most elegant females, I felt fat, forty, and somewhat futile. . . .

I looked around at the beautiful, exclusive-like creature who had just made her entrance, from an exclusive car, into that exclusive place and was about to order some of their exclusive food at a definitely exclusive price. Suddenly and unexpectedly the Eternal enquired of me, "Why do you think everyone is so tense?"

I discovered myself in a still point. "Competition," I replied with sudden comprehension. "That's right," He answered. It was very, very still in my heart and so I very distinctly heard the Eternal's next words: "Jill, you'll NEVER be competition." That was it—I WAS FREE! Oh, the joy of it. It was true! I could be a big sister to them, a friendly mother to them, an ugly aunt to them. But certainly I could relax knowing I would never threaten one of them. They were bound to listen to me for the very reason I had believed them bound not to. What an incredible release.

God had made me just right for my vocation and that was all that mattered. He had gifted me with ordinary and acceptable good looks. Everywhere I went someone would come up to me and tell me I was like their daughter, cousin, or Great Aunt Susan. Now I could see how comfortable that made everybody feel. Why, I was as familiar as family, and instead of being offended by these remarks, conjuring up freaky pictures of Great Aunt Frankenstein Susan, I was able to giggle and be content. I thanked Him for dressing me well enough to hold my own, but not too well to distract or cause envy, freeing me up in that moment of time to wear an outfit twice in a row if I wanted to, and not be trapped in an expensive game of "beat the fashion." . . .

To discover you are "just right" in His eyes is enough. *He* is the lover of our souls and to despise the way He has assembled our bodies, dressed our heads with foliage, or arranged our features, is to miss the point. To be able to say, I am free, not to be the "me" that "I" would choose to be, but the me "He" has already chosen me to be, is freedom indeed. . . .

As I kneeled, the Father dressed my spirit with an incredibly tender anticipation of Heavenly delight, and I told the Lord Jesus how much I loved Him for it all—He Who must have been tempted to be afraid so many, many times. . . .

The next time some dear little blue-haired ladies in tennis shoes came and whispered in my ear, "We couldn't hear you," and I asked, "Where were you sitting" and they answered me, "On the back row and we're all deaf you know," I found a sweet warmth and loving concern instead of the old irritation as I patiently suggested they sit on the front row next time.

It was all different. Women were everywhere. In my head and in my heart, in my plans and in my thinking, in my schedules and spare moments, on the phone and in my car, at the restaurant, and at tennis, in my tears and in my laughter—they were part of me and I was part and parcel of them and I was *glad, glad, glad*—we were women together.

Chapter Seven
PEACE FROM FAITH

And the peace of God, which passeth all understanding, shall keep your hearts and minds through Christ Jesus.

—PHILIPPIANS 4:7

As the moon rises over Monument Valley, Arizona, the whole world seems at peace.

Delicately colored irises cover the bank of the Upper Deschutes River, Deschutes National Forest, Oregon.

CHRIST STILLING THE TEMPEST

Fear was within the tossing bark
When stormy winds grew loud;
And waves came rolling high and dark,
And the tall mast was bowed.

And men stood breathless in their dread
And baffled in their skill,
But One was there who rose and said
To the wild sea, "Be still!"

And the wind ceased—it ceased!—that word
Passed through the gloomy sky;
The troubled billows knew their Lord
And sank beneath His eye.

And slumber settled on the deep
And silence on the blast,
As when the righteous falls asleep
When death's fierce throes are past.

Thou that didst rule the angry hour
And tame the tempest's mood,
Oh, send Thy spirit forth in power
O'er our dark souls to brood!

Thou that didst bow the billows' pride
Thy mandates to fulfill,
Speak, speak, to passion's raging tide,
Speak and say, "Peace, be still!"

FELICIA DOROTHEA HEMANS

OF PEACE AND LOVE

FIRST EPISTLE OF CLEMENT

*L*et us fix our eyes on the Father and Creator of the whole world and hold fast to His excellent gifts of peace and love. Let us contemplate His purposes in creation and consider how free from all anger He is towards His creatures. The moon and stars move in harmony, as He has ordered; day and night follow the course fixed by Him without hindering each other. The earth teems with all kinds of creatures and gives food in abundance for all as He has ordained. The sea is gathered in the places He has chosen and does not break through the shore and flood the dry land. The seasons of spring, summer, autumn, and winter give way to one another in peace. The winds blow from north, east, south, and west as He calls them, and springs of water break through the rocks to supply drink for animals and men. God in all His creation witted that there should be perfect peace and concord. And when mankind fell into sin, bringing conflict and misery, He sent His Son, Jesus Christ, to restore peace.

And he arose, and rebuked the wind, and said unto the sea, Peace, be still. And the wind ceased, and there was a great calm. And he said unto them, Why are ye so fearful? how is it that ye have no faith?
—MARK 4:39–40

PEACE FROM FAITH

143

WE SEE JESUS

I don't look back—God knows the fruitless efforts,
  The wasted hours, the sinning, the regrets;
I leave them all with Him Who blots the record
  And mercifully forgives and then forgets.

I don't look forward—God sees all the future,
  The road that, short or long, will lead me home;
And He will face with me its every trial
  And bear for me the burdens that may come.

I don't look round me—then would fears assail me,
  So wild the tumult of earth's restless seas,
So dark the world, so filled with woe and evil,
  So vain the hope of comfort or ease.

I don't look in—for then am I most wretched;
  Myself has naught on which to stay my trust.
Nothing I see save failures and short-comings
  And weak endeavors crumbling into dust.

But I look up—into the face of Jesus,
  For there my heart can rest, my fears are stilled;
And there is joy and love and light for darkness
  And perfect peace, and every hope fulfilled.
ANNIE JOHNSON FLINT

---

*. . . be of good comfort, be of one
mind, live in peace; and the God of
love and peace shall be with you.*

—2 CORINTHIANS 13:11

At sunset, the sailboats
have come to safe harbor
in Morro Bay, California.

O Lord, support us all the day long until the shadows lengthen and the evening comes, and the busy world is hushed, and the fever of life is over, and our work is done. Then, Lord, in Your mercy, grant us safe lodging and a holy rest and peace at the last through Jesus Christ our Lord. Amen.

JOHN HENRY NEWMAN

PRAYERS OF PEACE

And as they thus spake, Jesus himself stood in the midst of them, and saith unto them, Peace be unto you.

—LUKE 24:36

My Lord, God, I have no idea where I am going. I do not see the road ahead of me. I cannot know for certain where it will end. Nor do I really know myself, and the fact that I think I am following Your will does not mean that I am actually doing so. But I believe that the desire to please You does in fact please You. And I hope I have that desire in all that I am doing. I hope that I will never do anything apart from that desire. And I know that if I do this, You will lead me by the right road, though I may know nothing about it. Therefore, will I trust You always though I may seem to be lost in the shadow of death. I will not fear for You are ever with me, and You will never leave me to face my perils alone.

THOMAS MERTON

Father, I know now, if I never knew it before, that only in Thee can my restless human heart find any peace.

For I began life without knowledge but full of needs. And the turmoil of my mind, the dissatisfaction of my life all stem from trying to meet those needs with the wrong things and in the wrong places.

Help me so to live that my conscience shall not have to accuse, so that I may be saved the necessity of trying to mend that which need never be broken. I know that only then will the civil war within me cease.

May I be willing to have Thee with me in play as well as in work, knowing that with Thee I shall have peace and joy and no regrets. Through Jesus Christ, my Lord. Amen.

PETER MARSHALL

Lord, make me an instrument of Your peace. Where there is hatred, let me sow love; where there is injury, pardon; where there is doubt, faith; where there is despair, hope; where there is darkness, light; where there is sadness, joy. O Divine Master, grant that I may not so much seek to be consoled as to console, not so much to be understood as to understand, not so much to be loved as to love; for it is in giving that we receive, it is in pardoning that we are pardoned, it is in dying that we awake to eternal life.

SAINT FRANCIS OF ASSISI

Lord, give us peace in our days, for there is none that fighteth for us but Thou alone, our God. Lord, peace be made in Thy strength and plenty in Thy towers. God, of whom be holy desires, rightful counsels and just deeds, give to Thy servants that peace that the world may not give, so that our hearts may be given to keep Thine hests and dread of our enemies may be taken from us, so that our times may be peaceable by Thy protection, by our Lord Jesus Christ Thy Son, that liveth with Thee and reigneth God, by all worlds of worlds.

MS. DOUCE

FOOTPATH TO PEACE

HENRY VAN DYKE

To be glad of life because it gives you the chance to love and to work and to play and to look up at the stars; to be satisfied with your possessions but not contented with yourself until you have made the best of them; to despise nothing in the world except falsehood and meanness and to fear nothing except cowardice; to be governed by your admirations rather than by your disgusts; to covet nothing that is your neighbor's except his kindness of heart and gentleness of manners; to think seldom of your enemies, often of your friends, and every day of Christ; and to spend as much time as you can, with body and with spirit, in God's out-of-doors—these are little guideposts on the footpath to peace.

JOY AND PEACE IN BELIEVING

Sometimes a light surprises
The Christian when he sings;
It is the Lord who rises
With healing on His wings.
When comforts are declining,
He brands the soul again,
A season of clear shining
To cheer it after rain.

In holy contemplation
We sweetly then pursue
The theme of God's salvation
And find it ever new.

Set free from present sorrow,
We cheerfully can say,
Let the unknown tomorrow
Bring with it what it may!

It can bring with it nothing
But He will bear us through;
Who gives the lilies clothing
Will clothe His people too.
Beneath the spreading Heavens
No creature but is fed;
And He who feeds the ravens
Will give His children bread.

WILLIAM COWPER

A still lake reflects the snow-covered majesty of Mount Ranier in Washington.

PEACE FROM FAITH

VISION OF THE SPIRIT

HELEN KELLER

As I wander through the dark, encountering difficulties, I am aware of encouraging voices that murmur from the spirit realm. I sense a holy passion pouring down from the springs of Infinity. I thrill to music that beats with the pulses of God. Bound to suns and planets by invisible cords, I feel the flame of eternity in my soul. Here, in the midst of the everyday air, I sense the rush of ethereal rains. I am conscious of the splendour that binds all things of earth to all things of Heaven—immured by silence and darkness, I possess the light which shall give me vision a thousand-fold when death sets me free.

O MASTER, LET ME WALK WITH THEE

O Master, let me walk with Thee
In lowly paths of service free.
Tell me Thy secret; help me bear
The strain of toil, the fret of care.

Help me the slow of heart to move
By some clear, winning word of love;
Teach me the wayward feet to stay
And guide them in the homeward way.

In hope that sends a shining ray
Far down the future's broadening way,
In peace that only Thou canst give,
With Thee, O Master, let me live!

WASHINGTON GLADDEN

THOU ART NEAR

O light-bringer of my blindness,
O spirit never far removed!
Ever when the hour of travail deepens,
Thou art near;
Set in my soul like jewels bright
Thy words of holy meaning,
Till Death with gentle hand shall lead me
To the Presence I have loved—
My torch in darkness here,
My joy eternal there.

HELEN KELLER

A radiant sunset streaks
the sky over the North
and Middle Sister
Mountains in McKenzie
Pass, Oregon.

SWEET PEACE, THE GIFT OF GOD'S LOVE

Peter P. Bilhorn, 1861-1936

Peter P. Bilhorn, 1861-1936

1. There comes to my heart one sweet strain, (sweet strain,) A
2. Thro' Christ on the cross peace was made, (was made,) My
3. When Je - sus as Lord I had crowned, (had crowned,) My
4. In Je - sus for peace I a - bide, (a - bide,) And

glad and a joy - ous re - frain; (re - frain;) I sing it a -
debt by His death was all paid; (all paid;) No oth - er foun -
heart with this peace did a - bound; (a - bound;) In Him the rich
as I keep close to His side, (His side,) There's noth - ing but

gain and a - gain, Sweet peace, the gift of God's love.
da - tion is laid For peace, the gift of God's love.
bless - ing I found, Sweet peace, the gift of God's love.
peace doth be - tide, Sweet peace, the gift of God's love.

WALKING ON THE SEA

When the storm on the mountains of Galilee fell
And lifted its water on high,
And the faithless disciples were bound in the spell
Of mysterious alarm—their terrors to quell,
Jesus whispered, "Fear not, it is I."

The storm could not bury that word in the wave,
For 'twas taught through the tempest to fly;
It shall reach His disciples in every clime,
And His voice shall be near in each troublous time,
Saying, "Be not afraid, it is I."

When the spirit is broken with sickness or sorrow
And comfort is ready to die,
The darkness shall pass; and in gladness tomorrow,
The wounded complete consolation shall borrow
From his life-giving word, "It is I."

When the waters are passed and the glories unknown
Burst forth on the wondering eye,
The compassionate "Lamb in the midst of the throne"
Shall welcome, encourage, and comfort his own
And say, "Be not afraid, it is I."

NATHANIEL HAWTHORNE

Then the same day at evening, being the first day of the week . . . came Jesus and stood in the midst, and saith unto them, Peace be unto you.

—JOHN 20:19

*Fog rolling in at dawn provides a moment of
peace in the Kalamath Marsh of Oregon.*

UP-HILL

Does the road wind up-hill all the way?
 Yes, to the very end.
Will the day's journey take the whole long day?
 From morn to night, my friend.

But is there for the night a resting-place?
 A roof for when the slow, dark hours begin.
May not the darkness hide it from my face?
 You cannot miss that inn.

Shall I meet other wayfarers at night?
 Those who have gone before.
Then must I knock or call when just in sight?
 They will not keep you standing at that door.

Shall I find comfort, travel-sore and weak?
 Of labour you shall find the sum.
Will there be beds for me and all who seek?
 Yea, beds for all who come.

CHRISTINA GEORGINA ROSSETTI

These things I have spoken unto you, that in me ye might have peace. In the world ye shall have tribulation: but be of good cheer; I have overcome the world.

—JOHN 16:33

PEACE

Peace is gazing into depths
Of water, cool and clear,
And knowing fast within your heart
That God is ever near.

Peace is living day by day
With His own company,
So you will have within your soul
Divine tranquility.

MILDRED SPIRES JACOBS

ALL THROUGH THE NIGHT

Sleep, my love, and peace attend thee,
All through the night;
Guardian angels God will lend thee,
All through the night;
Soft the drowsy hours are creeping,
Hill and dale in slumber steeping,
Love alone his watch is keeping—
All through the night.

Hark! a solemn bell is ringing,
Clear through the night;
Thou, my love, art heavenward winging,
Home through the night;
Earthly dust from off thee shaken,
Soul immortal thou shalt waken,
With thy last dim journey taken—
Home through the night.

AUTHOR UNKNOWN

At dusk, the sun lingers over the buttes that line the Crooked River in Oregon.

PEACE FROM FAITH

ENTERING IN

CATHERINE MARSHALL

n March 1943 came the event that was to change my life. A routine physical check-up brought bad news. Chest x-rays showed a soft spotting over both lungs. Specialists were unable to make a conclusive diagnosis, but the trouble appeared to be tuberculosis. Tuberculosis! Hated word, hated disease. I was ordered to bed twenty-four hours a day for an indefinite period. . . .

Despair settled in. After almost a year and a half in bed, I could see few gains. My husband and four-year-old son needed me. Our household situation was becoming more difficult with every month that passed. . . .

There was in me a desire for an all-out effort to reach Him, born of desperation. Sloughed off now were all the trappings of religion, most of them concerned with the ceremonial or organizational aspects of churches that so often confuse the central issue. I began to see wholeness as more than the search for physical health. As I understood the viewpoint of Jesus, it was that physical soundness is merely part of a more profound wholeness. In this sense, wholeness can

only come about as inner cleavages are healed, as man is joined to the Source of his being. Thus, for me, the search for health became a search for a relationship with God. The question was, what was blocking that relationship? . . .

So that sunshiny June morning, I got out of bed and stood at the bedroom window looking out at the garden that Peter had so lovingly planted. . . . A blue, blue sky above . . . The sea just over the brow of the hill. There I stood and took the plunge. It amounted to a quiet pledge to God, the promise of a blank check with my life:

"It is ten-twelve A.M. on the twenty-second of June 1944," I said. "From this moment I promise that I'll try to do whatever You tell me for the rest of my life, insofar as You'll make it clear to me what Your wishes are. I'm weak and many times I'll probably want to renege on this. But Lord, You'll have to help me with that too."

I took a deep breath; I was trembling. I had entered in. Yet nothing seemed different. The hollyhock faces still nodded at the window. Fluffy clouds still floated in that blue, blue sky. I turned and noted in my

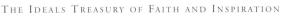

The serenity of Bow Lake reflects the clouds at sunrise in Banff National Park, Canada.

journal the date and the hour of the promise I had just made. There would be moments in the future when this pledge would not seem real to me. But it was real, and writing it down would help to remind me.

I felt no emotion other than the relief of knowing that I had completed my part, so far as I knew it. This brought me a peace of mind I had not known during the tortuous days of self-probing and writing the letters of confession.

The proof of the reality of the pledge I had made began coming during the next six weeks. My physical condition was improving. Each morning I would lie in the yard, soaking up the sunshine. Next I tried joining the family for dinner each night. That did not tire me over much. Then I began taking short walks some afternoons with Jeffrey, our cocker spaniel, trotting beside me. It was a joy to stand at the top of the rise in the road and see the sea again, feel the tangy salt air on my cheeks. . . . It was even good to feel sand in my shoes. As of old, I began taking an interest in the garden and the kitchen. . . . It was like coming to life again. And life was good, so good. The speck of light at the other end of the tunnel was becoming a steady beam.

INDEX

Accept Our Tribute, 99
All People That on Earth Do Dwell, 104
All through the Night, 157
Allen, James, 31
Anderson, Beverly J., 21
Anderson, Terry, 48
Aquinas, Thomas, 35
Aspects of Christianity, 23
Babcock, Maltbie Davenport, 31
Baker, Henry W., 134
Barclay, William, 56
Barton, Marie, 44
Be Strong, 31
Best Is Yet to Be, The, 114
Bilhorn, Peter P., 152
Bolton, Sarah K., 37
Bonar, Horatius, 77
Bonhoeffer, Dietrich, 39
Book of Common Prayer, 13, 80
Bowie, W. Russell, 81
Bradstreet, Anne, 84
Brent, Charles H., 81
Bridge Builder, The, 134
Briscoe, Jill, 136
Brontë, Emily, 31
Burket, Gail Brook, 35
Call, The, 128
Carey, Alice, 124
Christ Stilling the Tempest, 142
Christ with Me, Christ Before Me, 45
Clark, Thomas Curtis, 104
Courage, 31, 44
Cowper, William, 54, 149
Credo, 89
Crowell, Grace Noll, 11, 34, 89
Culver, Eleanor Lyons, 100
Daily Prayers Dissolve Your Cares, 8
Dawson, George, 35
Do Not Worry about Your Life, 39
Douce, MS., 147
Dromgoole, Will Allen, 134
Earle, John Charles, 77
Elliott, Charlotte, 95
Entering In, 158
Epistle of Barnabas, 23
Evidence Not Seen, 24
Faith, 2
Faith of a Mariner, The, 64
Father, Take My Hand, 53
Finding Happiness, 42
First Epistle of Clement, 143
Flint, Annie Johnson, 17, 144
Footpath to Peace, 149
Footprints, 47
Foundations of Faith, 133
Frank, Anne, 42
Frere, Walter Howard, 56
Gannett, William Channing, 20
Gladden, Washington, 150
God Give Me Joy, 104
God Knows, 59
God Means Us to Be Happy, 89
God Will Deliver, 23
God's Grandeur, 100
God's World, 107
Grace of God, The, 20
Hall, Myrtle, 90

Hawthorne, Nathaniel, 155
He Leads Me On, 44
He Keeps the Key, 54
Hemans, Felicia Dorothea, 142
Herbert, Mary Sidney, 8
Herbert, George, 123, 128
Heroes of Faith, 67
Hickok, Eliza M., 80
Hinckley, Mabel Demers, 44
Hope, 11, 21
Hope Dwells Ever in the Soul, 14
Hopkins, Gerard Manley, 100
How We Bought L'Abri, 70
I Believe, 68
I Heard Him, 100
I Heard the Voice of Jesus Say, 77
Immortal Love, Forever Full, 128
Increasing Love, 122
Jacobs, Mildred Spires, 157
Jarrett, Bede, 11
Joy and Peace in Believing, 149
Joy of Friendship, The, 112
Joyful, Joyful, We Adore Thee, 108
Keeling, Mildred, 107
Keller, Helen, 150
Kempis, Thomas à, 57, 61, 121
Kennedy, Pamela, 112
Kethe, William, 104
King of Love My Shepherd Is, The, 134
Lamp of Faith, The, 31
Lawrence, J. B., 68
Life Heroic, A, 37
Life's Lessons, 78
Light Shining out of Darkness, 54
Like a Candle, 44
Lo, I Am with You Always, 77
Longfellow, Henry Wadsworth, 37
Look on the Sunny Side, 65
Lord's Leading, The, 32
Love Bade Me Welcome, 123
Love Lifted Me, 130
Love Passes through All, 121
Love's Prerogative, 127
Luther, Martin, 57
Marshall, Catherine, 92, 158
Marshall, Peter, 34, 147
Melanchthon, Philipp, 103
Merton,Thomas, 102, 146
Mighty Fortress Is Our God, A, 40
My Faith Looks Up to Thee, 86
My Lord and My All, 95
Neumann, Casper, 81
New Day, A, 90
Newman, John Henry, 146
Newton, John, 95
O Holy Saviour, Friend Unseen, 95
O Master, Let Me Walk with Thee, 150
Of Peace and Love, 143
Olson, Enid Martell, 12
Orchard, William E., 13
Our Endless Home, 11
Oxenham, John, 2, 89, 127
Palmerston, June, 44
Peace, 157
Powers, Margaret Fishback, 47
Praise to the Creator, 99

Prayer, 65
Prayers for Comfort, 80
Prayers for Courage, 34
Prayers for Hope, 12
Prayers of Joy, 102
Prayers of Love, 124
Prayers of Peace, 146
Prayers of Trust, 56
Proctor, Adelaide A., 103
Psalm of Life, A, 37
Psalm Twenty-three, 42
Rice, Helen Steiner, 8, 65
Riley, James Whitcomb, 125
Robbins, Samuel Dowse, 53
Rose, Darlene Deibler, 24
Rossetti, Christina Georgina, 157
Saint Anselm, 103, 125
Saint Birgitta, 102
Saint Francis de Sales, 23
Saint Francis of Assisi, 81, 147
Saint Patrick, 45
Saving Faith through Trust, 53
Schaeffer, Edith, 70
Seventy-First Psalm, The, 8
Simsic, Wayne, 133
Small Graces, 48
Solid Rock, The, 18
Spurgeon, Charles, 53, 64
Stead, Louisa M. R., 62
Stidger, William L., 133
Stream of Faith, The, 20
Strong, Patience, 14, 21
Sun on Stone, 21
Sweet Peace, the Gift of God's Love, 152
Taize Community, 103
ten Boom, Corrie, 114
Tennyson, Alfred, Lord, 14
Therefore Give Us Love, 121
Thou Art Near, 150
Three Lessons, 38
'Tis So Sweet to Trust in Jesus, 62
To Comfort All That Mourn, 92
To One in Sorrow, 89
Today, 127
Tolstoy, Leo, 122
Trust, 61
Ultra-suede Ladies, The, 136
Up-Hill, 157
Upon the Burning of Our House, 84
Van Dyke, Henry, 149
Vision of the Spirit, 150
von Schiller, Johann Christoph Friedrich, 38
Walking on the Sea, 155
Watts, Isaac, 20, 99
We Trust, 14
We See Jesus, 144
What God Hath Promised, 17
Whatever Is, Is Best, 83
When Is the Time to Trust?, 60
Whittier, John Greenleaf, 128
Who Will Lead Me into Edom?, 133
Wilcox, Ella Wheeler, 83
Wordsworth, Christopher, 121
Ye Heavens, Uplift Your Voice, 110

THE IDEALS TREASURY OF FAITH AND INSPIRATION